INCURABLE

By

Rita Doyle Walsh

Dedication

I dedicate this story,

To my son Philip J. Webb

For all of your struggles to stay alive.

I love you with all of my heart and soul

incurable

[in-**kyoo** r-*uh*-b*uh* l]

Spell Syllables

adjective

1.

not curable; that cannot be cured, remedied, or corrected:

an incurable disease.

2.

not susceptible to change:

his incurable pessimism.

noun

3.

a person suffering from an incurable disease.

Definition by GOOGLE

PROLOGUE

It was September 20, 2014, just an average Saturday for most people. Emma sat in the faux leather chair beside her son's hospital bed and stared out the window, seeing nothing. She was just staring off into space. Her body was exhausted and her mind was numb. Her eyelids felt like they were lined with sandpaper from all the tears she had recently shed and all of the hours she had gone without sleep.

Dr. Tessler walked up beside her, resting his hand on her shoulder. She never heard him enter the room in his booty covered soft soled shoes.

"Go home, Emma. Get some rest. There is nothing you can do right now." He spoke to her softly, so as not to disturb her son.

Emma patted his hand that still rested on her shoulder and smiled, grateful for his concern. The doctor knew Emma would not leave her son alone.

"His wife will be in shortly, as soon as she can locate a babysitter. I'll go home to rest then. Thanks Doc.".

The doctor nodded then checked Donnie's vitals. Nothing had changed. He slipped out of room 812 just as quietly as he had entered.

Keck Hospital at USC opened its doors in 1991. It was an ulta-modern facility and specialized in transplants of all kinds. The eighth floor was dedicated to patients with Cystic Fibrosis. It was located in the heart of Los Angeles, California.

Donnie stirred, groaned and took a few deep breaths from the oxygen mask covering his face. His eyes fluttered open for a minute. He saw his mother sitting there and she smiled at him. His eyes moved to look at the clock on the wall above Emma's head and he motioned with his head for her to look at the time. He smiled, closed his eyes and drifted back to sleep. It was 7:14 in the morning.

Emma's eyes closed involuntarily as she had spent the entire night at her son's bedside. She began to think about the little number game she played with her son so many years before. Donnie was born on July 14th, 1979. He weighed seven pounds and fourteen ounces. So that became Emma's new lucky number, 714. However, as her son grew, he too began to recognize that number as his favorite; it followed them both everywhere. The only place it never showed up, they would joke with one another, was in the lottery. Emma drifted off to sleep, sitting up in the chair she had occupied all night long. She began to dream and memories came flooding back.

Chapter 1

It was December 9, 1978 and it was Emma's fourth anniversary with her husband, Rick Clark. They had been high school sweethearts who got married right out of high school when they were both only 18. They had their first child, a little girl, before their first anniversary and one year and five days later, they had their second daughter. That baby, Katie, was now two years old and her sister Jessie was three.

Emma went to the hairdressers that morning for a new hairdo. This was a very special occasion. Rick made reservations for dinner at a new restaurant that had recently opened in the harbor by the marina. It was a bit extravagant for their budget but it was their wedding anniversary. Emma had a great surprise for her husband. She wanted to look her very best.

Rick was a fireman in town, following in his own father's footsteps. He was also a paramedic who had worked at that job for almost two years before this job opened up in town. He was still fairly new on the force but it was almost like finding a new family. They were a close bunch of guys and he loved the job.

Rick was supposed to have that Saturday off, however being the low man on the totem pole, when one of the older guys called in sick, Rick was called in to cover for him. But his shift was to end at four so he told Emma not to worry, it would not interfere with their six o'clock reservations.

Emma was talking on the phone to one of her closest friends, while doing her nails with the new polish she bought at the hair salon. It matched her soft pink angora dress perfectly. For December in New England, it was a nice day. It was chilly but the sun was shining. If it wasn't for the wind, it would have been a perfect day, Emma thought. It would be lovely sitting by one of those large windows that over looked Plymouth harbor. Even though it was early December, so many people already had their Christmas lights up including the restaurants by the water. It was such a festive time of year. She and Ricky both loved the month of December, that's why they decided to get married at that time of year. People called them crazy but they were so compatible.

"Hey Diane, I really need to get going," Emma told her friend over the phone. "Rick should be home already. I wonder what is keeping him. I'll talk to you tomorrow and tell you all about our dinner at Harbor One."

Emma blew on her wet polished nails and shook them to help them dry quickly. It was four thirty. Rick should be pulling into the drive way any second. She had ironed one of his good shirts and made sure his trousers were neat and clean. She picked out a nice sweater for him to wear that would go well with the tie she bought him last Christmas. Rick wasn't much of a "tie" man, more of a jeans and sweatshirt kind of guy. But he sure did clean up pretty, she thought to herself.

At four fifty, Emma began to pace, wondering what was keeping her husband. She knew that he was looking forward to their anniversary dinner just as much as she was. If they didn't have plans, she might not have been so concerned but he promised her that he'd come right home and not stop off to have a drink with the guys like he did on some occasions.

At five o'clock Emma called the girls to come out of their room and have dinner, macaroni and cheese, which they loved. She cut a boiled hot dog in half for each of them, removed the skin and served it on the same plate in bite size pieces for her little girls.

At five past five, with her nerves on edge, she picked up the phone to call Rick at the station. She didn't want to act like a nagging wife but she was concerned. The babysitter was due to arrive at five thirty.

"Hi Sally. This is Emma Clark. Is Rick still there by any chance?" She said timidly, hoping Sally, the dispatcher, wouldn't think she was meddling.

"Oh gosh, Emma. There was an explosion up on Pond Street and three houses caught on fire. That was about two thirty. The guys have not got it contained yet. I think it was a gas line explosion so this could take some time. I haven't heard any reports yet but when I do, I'll keep you posted."

Emma's heart dropped. She thanked Sally and hung up the phone. Feeling a little dejected at first, but then worry replaced that emotion. They could go out to dinner anytime. It was just that she had

such a great surprise for Rick. She was going to have another baby.

Maybe this time, it would be a son.

Chapter 2

Emma called one of the wives of a man she knew was working with Rick. The woman said she was worried. She had a scanner and had been listening to what was going on and it didn't look good. She asked Emma if she wanted to go with her to go check it out. They probably couldn't get too close, since it was a gas explosion, but the two wives just needed to make sure that their husbands were okay. The gal told her she could pick her up at five thirty. The babysitter would be there by then so Emma agreed to go.

Emma still dressed in her jeans, threw on her boots and a light weight winter jacket and once the babysitter was settled, Emma walked to the end of her driveway just as Maddie pulled up in front of her house. Madelyn Jeffers was a bit older than Emma and she had been married for over six years. She had two children and a mother-in-law who lived with them. She often joked about having a built in babysitter, but the truth be known, the woman was a godsend. She cooked and cleaned and shopped and did laundry while Maddie worked full time as a nurse in a doctor's private practice.

The wives had to park several streets over from Pond Street and walk through back yards and driveways to get closer. There were people everywhere, policemen trying to keep the spectators back. The gas company was there, and everything had been turned off but there was always still a danger. But even with all that going on, Maddie knew there was an undercurrent of pandemonium. Something had happened beyond the fire.

An ambulance came up the road, trying to get by all the fire trucks. Its clamoring siren finally shut down. The driver and two paramedics jumped out, pulling the stretcher out from the back of the truck.

Oh yes, Maddie nodded. She turned to Emma to tell her she just knew someone was injured. They held hands and said silent prayers to themselves. Please dear Lord, don't let it be my husband.

Maddie's husband came out of a burning house, covered in soot and he saw his wife standing there with Emma. He jogged over to them. Maddie breathed a sigh of relief. She was glad to see him unhurt.

"Maddie, I've asked you not to come to these fires." You could see the distress on his handsome, dirty face. Then he turned to Emma.

"Emma, I'm so sorry. It's Rick. He fell through the floor on the second level and crashed through the timbers, all the way to the basement. We are trying to get him out. He's semi conscious, but you should not be here." He turned to his wife. "Please take her home and stay with her. I'll call you as soon as I know more."

Emma shook her head…no way was she leaving. Tears flooded her eyes. "It's our anniversary." She just blurted out the first thing that came to mind. "I'm going to have another baby." She said in almost a whisper, to anyone who was listening. Maggie put her arms around her friend and hugged her tight. "Please God, make him be okay."

"Oh Emma. He'll be okay. He will." She tried to believe that herself. Bill Jeffers left the women to return to the problems at hand. Donnie's father died without ever knowing that he was going to have a son.

Chapter 3

After Rick's death, his family from the firehouse rallied around Emma. She was pregnant and had two small children to take care of and now she was a widow. They made sure her driveway got plowed when it snowed and that she had firewood for the fireplace and no problems with her house. Whenever she had a leak or malfunction, one of the firemen made sure it got fixed for her.

Maddie offered to be her coach when she delivered the baby and she was a huge help, having two children of her own plus being a nurse. Her friend Diane, who was still single, would drop by unannounced to take her out to a movie, or to go for a bite to eat or sometimes just to babysit to let Emma get out alone to shop or do errands.

The wives of the firemen had given her one of the nicest baby showers anyone could expect; she wanted for nothing. Nothing except for the father of her son, but that could never be. She took the loss hard, but when Donnie was born, it was like a light had been turned back on in her life. He was a beautiful little boy with blonde hair and dark brown eyes. Such a contrast made him even cuter. Emma was a strawberry blonde with hazel eyes. Rick had been darker in complexion with dark brown hair and eyes of coal. They were so dark, Emma used to say that he had two black eyes.

Her friends were wonderful but it didn't replace her husband. Emma had her hands full. The nights were long and lonely. And Donnie demanded much of her time. He didn't sleep well. Every few hours he'd wake her up crying uncontrollably as if he was starving to death. His crying often woke one of the girls.

"Momma I want a drink of water. Why is he always crying?" Jessie said one night at two in the morning.

Emma dragged her weary bones out of bed, picked Donnie up from his crib, trying to ignore his screams, she fetched the water for her daughter, kissed her forehead and told her to go back to sleep.

She walked to the kitchen turning on the light, pulled the formula filled bottle from the refrigerator and put it into the small saucepan full of water that still sat on the stove from his last feeding, three hours prior.

While it heated up she would carry Donnie to the sofa and change his diaper. His little face was flushed as if he had a fever and his hair was soaking wet from fussing so much. She picked him up thinking his belly was hard and seemed full, why was he always so hungry? For all the times he ate, he didn't seem to be growing very much.

She pulled the bottle from the boiling water and tested it, now it was too hot. She sighed as she ran it under cold water as he continued to cry in her arms.

Emma bounced her son on her hip, trying to placate him but it was no use. The only thing he wanted was his bottle. She carried it and him into the living room, turning on a small lamp on the table, sat down and fed her son. He gobbled it up.

"Oh my poor baby. You really were starving, weren't you?" she whispered, looking into his beautiful little face.

She sat him up on her lap, getting ready to burp him when he vomited. The whole four ounces erupted like a fountain across the room, covering Emma and him, along with the couch and the rug.

"Oh dear heaven above, Donnie. What is the matter poor baby?"

Instantly he began to scream again, crying so loud that both of his sisters were now out of bed and standing in the hallway.

"What's the matter with him mommy?" Katie asked. "Oh yuk, he threw up again."

Tears streamed down Emma's face. She was too exhausted to endure much more of this. But she had no one to help her.

"Go back to bed girls, please." Emma begged.

"Can we sleep in your bed Momma?" Jessie asked pleadingly.

"Sure, go ahead. I don't know when I'll ever get some sleep. Scoot."

The girls ran down the hallway and hopped up into their mother's bed, giggling and talking but soon, they were fast asleep.

Emma changed the baby and put him down to throw on some fresh pajamas, dropping her vomit covered nightgown into the hamper along with his pajamas. She went back to the kitchen to heat up another bottle for her screaming baby boy. She fed him only one ounce at a time, burping him in between each ounce in spite of his fussing for more food. Finally three ounces down and he fell back to sleep. She quietly tiptoed into his room and placed him into his crib, pulled up the blanket and kissed his head.

"Please sleep until the sun comes up, little guy. Please sleep."

She peeked in at her two daughters cuddled close together, sound asleep. She fixed the blanket so they'd both be warm and she retreated into Jessie's little twin bed.

At Donnie's 3 month check up with her pediatrician, the doctor noted that he had the beginning of a cold, which was most unusual for a baby of that young age. He also noted that Donnie was not growing at the normal rate and asked how well he had been tolerating the formula. Emma explained that he ate very fast but often ended up vomiting when she tried to burp him. He'd cry like he was still hungry so she'd feed him again but after a few ounces, he'd fall back to sleep. The doctor told her to keep an eye on him and call if his cold got suddenly worse.

A week later, Donnie was admitted to the hospital with

pneumonia. They had to put an IV in his little ankle. He was still so small. Ten days later he was released only to be readmitted with another bout of pneumonia a day before Thanksgiving. At four months of age, Donnie was still only around eight pounds, very small for his age. His stomach was hard and distended and he was literally starving to death. Even with a big round stomach, you could count his ribs. His arms and legs were like sticks. Every time she fed him now, he would vomit across the room; called projectile vomiting her pediatrician informed her. Then he'd scream in pain, looking for more to eat. Emma was at her wits end.

When the local hospital did all the tests they were equipped to do, Maddie went with Emma to transport Donnie to The Floating Hospital for Women and Children in Boston. Donnie's doctor knew someone on staff there and asked him to perform further testing on the young child. Her friend Diane babysat for the girls.

Emma was interrogated by a team of doctors asking her questions about her own health, that of the father and they asked questions about her pregnancy. They wanted to know family history.

Her mother had died from breast cancer at the age of fifty two. Her father was well and living on Cape Cod. As far as she knew, he had no ailments, took no medications. She was an only child, as was Rick. His parents were both deceased. His mother was killed in an automobile accident and his father died from lung cancer. He was a big smoker plus being a fireman. By the time Maggie drove Emma back home to Plymouth, almost an hour's drive in heavy traffic, they were both exhausted. Maddie picked up some Kentucky Fried Chicken to bring home to her family for dinner. She invited Emma to join them, but Emma was in no mood to eat. Her baby was very ill and all alone in a hospital up in Boston. Diane had fed the girls pancakes with blueberries and had some left over for Emma when she got home. Diane was not big on cooking since she was single, worked full time and travelled in her job. She ate out a lot.

Diane stayed for a while to help get the girls bathed and into bed. She could see that Emma was just drained and very worried. She poured them each a glass of wine and laughed when Emma picked up a cold pancake and snacked on it, drinking white wine.

The next morning Emma woke early. She took a hot shower and got dressed then woke her girls.

"Let's go visit Grampa," she told them to hurry them along getting dressed. She made them some oatmeal and then they all hopped into her car and drove half an hour down to the Cape to visit with her father to tell him about little Donnie.

Frank McNally, or Mack as everyone called him, owned his own little deli style restaurant. He opened at seven in the morning for breakfast, did lunch and early bird dinners. He closed at seven at night, seven days a week. Seven to Seven for Seven. Emma couldn't remember the last time her father took a vacation or even a full day off. He loved what he did. He lived in the apartment upstairs over the deli. He and his wife opened the place twenty years ago. Once she passed on, people thought he might sell the place but he had nowhere to go and nothing to do, so he kept it to stay busy and it still thrived today.

Being a Saturday the place was already busy when Emma and the girls arrived just before eight. She walked up to the ten stool counter and picked up a menu. She ordered a cup of coffee, black and when she put the menu down, her father saw her from the kitchen. He smiled and left his spot at the expediting station and walked out to give his only daughter and granddaughters a big hug and a kiss.

"Well, well, my sweet redhead. What brings you to Mack's Deli on a fine Saturday morning?' He sat down on the stool beside her.

"Have you got a few minutes dad? Can we move to a table?"

Mack told the waitress to bring him a coffee and they'd move to a table. Papa helped the girls up onto booster seats and pushed their chairs in, kissing each one on the top of their heads. He noticed that Emma's eyes were red from crying. She looked lost and serious.

"What's wrong honey? Where's the baby?" Dad asked before taking a sip of his coffee.

Emma explained. Her eyes began to tear up again and she wiped them with a napkin, not wanting anyone to see her cry. Her father was very emotional and he got all choked up. His only child's baby; his only grandson was gravely ill and no one knew why.

"Emma, when are you going back to see him?' Dad wanted to

go with her.

She explained that she was told to wait for forty eight hours at least. They needed to do testing and get the child comfortable. They told her she could visit Donnie Sunday afternoon. Mack said he would pick her up at one and they'd go together. Emma was relieved. Her father seldom took time away from the deli but this was important. Diane said that she'd take the girls over to her house for the day.

That evening a cold front moved in and there was a frost in the morning. The day was dark and gloomy and very cold. Emma's mood matched the weather. She turned the heat up and dressed warm but she could not shake the cold that was in her bones.

Diane arrived bearing donuts and hot coffee from Dunkin Donuts. The smell filled the air the minute she walked through the door. She had donut holes for the girls and they were delighted. Emma made them hot chocolate with whipped cream. Diane told the girls to pack a knapsack with some toys and a change of clothes in case they wanted to stay overnight. They giggled with delight. Diane kissed Emma's cheek and told her not to worry about the girls, just call her when she got home. Diane was a good friend.

Dad was right on time, beeped the horn as he pulled into her long driveway. He didn't want to stop and visit, nor go inside. Emma grabbed her coat and gloves, locked the door and joined her father in his old Buick. At least it was roasty toasty inside.

She told her father that she thought she should have received a call from the baby's doctor, but no one called. Weekends can be unpredictable.

Normally it was difficult to find a parking spot near the hospital but today, Mack found a spot right on the side street beside the huge building. They pulled up the collar on their coats, put on their gloves and bowed their heads into the wind and trudged up the little hill and around the corner to enter the hospital.

They took the elevator to the third floor, pediatrics. It was quiet. No doctors giving orders or nurses bumping into one another. It was a peaceful Sunday. They stopped at the nurses' station to ask which room Donnie was in and then they went to find him.

Emma entered the room and stopped dead in her tracks. She

backed up a few steps and looked at the room number.

"What's the matter, Em?" Her father asked, concerned.

"I'm just checking. She did say room three oh nine, right?" Her father nodded in agreement.

She went back inside to find a sleeping child in a crib, covered by a clear plastic tent like covering that had a mist blowing inside, covering the baby. She had to look twice. Is that Donnie? Is that my son? She wasn't so sure. He looked even smaller somehow.

Mack stood there, staring at the contraption containing his grandson.

"I'm going to go get the nurse, Dad. I'll be right back." Emma all but ran back to the nurse's station to inquire what was going on.

"Oh, Mrs. Clark, I am so very sorry, Didn't Dr. Zampini call you with the test results?" Somehow it fell through the cracks and no one informed Emma of anything.

"I will get the doctor on call to meet you in your son's room. He'll explain it all to you." The nurse was already dialing the phone before Emma left the desk.

Emma and her father stood at the side of the crib when little Donnie woke up and began to cry. It wasn't his regular howling type cry; it was more of a soft, sad whimper. She went to push back the plastic so she could pick him up when a big, heavy nurse came waddling into his room.

"I'll help you with that dear. Do you want to do his postural drainage?"

"What? I don't know what's going on." Emma explained. The nurse flushed with embarrassment.

At that precise moment, the doctor on call walked into the tiny cubicle of a room. He told the nurse to change the baby and put him back into the crib, then leave them alone. He instructed her to come back in about ten minutes. The nurse had the child changed into a new diaper and fresh, dry pajamas almost instantly. She put him back into the crib and Donnie never made a sound.

"Please have a seat," the doctor said, as he pulled over 2 chairs for Emma and her dad. He stood by the crib facing them. Then he apologized for them not being informed.

He was a young man of small stature, with a dark complexion and spoke with a heavy accent, maybe from India, Emma thought. She had to listen hard to understand him.

"We got the test results back yesterday." He began to tell them, nonchalantly. "Have you ever heard of Cystic Fibrosis?" He paused. When both Emma and Mack just stared back at him, not saying a word, he continued. "It is an *incurable* disease that affects the pancreas and the lungs; it is both a digestive and respiratory disorder. For a while, it can be controlled with medication and physical therapy but I'm sorry to say, most children with Cystic Fibrosis don't live much longer than fourteen years."

He continued to rattle on but Emma never heard another word. Tears flowed from her eyes as if they'd never stop. Her father reached for a box of tissues on the table, handed a few to his daughter and wiped his own tears away. When Emma began to sob, the doctor ended his sermon and again apologized and offered sympathy for what she must be going through right now. He suggested they go home and that the nurses will tend to her child. The doctor would certainly call her tomorrow. He left the room quickly.

Emma reached in to pick up her baby and cried while kissing him. Papa also kissed his sweet cheek.

"Emma. He tastes salty." She looked at her father. She thought that she was crazy because every time she kissed her son, she thought the same thing. Much later, Emma learned that one of the signs of a child with CF is that they taste salty because their bodies don't absorb it. They have no digestive enzymes. That's why he so often vomited. And mucous clogs their lungs making it difficult to breathe. There was so much to learn. So little time for Donnie. She lost her mother. She lost her husband. Now she was going to lose her only son. It was heart wrenching. How could God be so cruel? She thought.

They rode down the elevator in silence, tears still falling from her eyes, a tissue in her hand. They walked outside the doors into the street and were greeted by big white snowflakes that had already covered the street and sidewalk. Emma slipped as she was opening the passenger side door to her father's car and she went down onto her butt. She sat there, crying so hard, she was unable to get up. She wasn't hurt; she was just so beaten up by emotion, that she couldn't help herself.

Mack ran around to her side and reached down to help pull her up to her feet, where he hugged her and they cried together, as people walked by wondering what just happened.

They drove all the way home in total silence, on that snowy afternoon, as the darkness began to invade. They both were deep in thought. What was going to happen now? It was December 9, 1979. It would have been her fifth anniversary had Rick not been killed in that fire. Mack pulled into his daughter's driveway, gave her a sweet kiss and told her to call him if she needed him. Emma went up the stairs, fumbled with her keys to unlock the door, went inside, turned on the light, removed her coat and sat down to take off her boots. She looked up at the clock. It was 4:17.

Chapter 4

SEPTEMBER 20, 2014

Emma woke with a start. She looked at the clock. 7:41 a.m.

She shook her head. Those same three numbers. They mix and change

but those same three numbers haunted her back then and always, even

now. She reached up and felt her face. It was wet. She had been crying

in her sleep. And then she recalled dreaming about the day Donnie was

diagnosed. He was given fourteen years to live. Today he was thirty

five, married with two children. He had beaten the odds but still,

Emma was not ready to let him go. Not now, not ever. The only thing

that could save her son now was a donor for a double lung transplant.

Without a transplant it was just a matter of time, maybe months,

maybe only weeks, before her son, Donovan Richard Clark, would die.

And that old, long time feeling of guilt rushed in yet again. If only

Emma hadn't transferred those defective genes to her son, this would

not be happening. Of course her husband had the same defective gene

as well, but he was not around to feel the guilt; to watch their son suffer while struggling to breathe. That guilt remained on Emma's shoulders alone to bear. Both parents must have the defective gene in order to pass it on to their children. The problem was, you didn't know if you had that awful gene until a child was diagnosed with CF.

Donnie's wife, Olivia, arrived and put her arms around her mother-in-law, giving her a kiss on the cheek.

"Hi, Mom" she whispered with a soft smile. "Sorry it took me so long to get here. It's not easy to find a babysitter in the morning especially on Saturday." She explained.

"Hey, what are you two whispering about?" Donnie attempted to smile at his wife and mother, holding the oxygen mask above his face. "Mom go home. You make me tired looking at you." He was always teasing her, joking around as if there was nothing wrong. She loved him with all of her heart.

Emma kissed Donnie on his forehead, squeezed his hand and said she'd be back by five so Olivia could go home to the kids. She told Olivia to call her if she was needed. She left the hospital room and somehow made it to her car. She was on automatic pilot at that point as she drove home without any recollection of how she got there. She dropped her clothes on a chair in her bedroom and climbed under the covers. She was asleep in seconds.

Emma slept restlessly all day and woke with a start at four twenty in the afternoon.

She quickly took a shower to revive herself, grabbed a cup of coffee and a piece of toast with peanut butter on it and she was out the door by five. She told Donnie's wife that she'd be back by that time. She couldn't believe she slept so long. Olivia had the day time shift to sit with Donnie and Emma had the night. There was no one else to sit with Donnie and Emma didn't want him to ever be alone. What if…what if…she couldn't allow herself to finish that thought, she just didn't want him to be alone.

Olivia had taken a leave of absence from her part time job to be with her husband. She didn't expect that he'd be so ill and be in the hospital for such a long time. There was talk that he might never be released; he was there to wait for a donor. This wasn't like all the other times where he went in for a week or two for IV antibiotic treatments then released. This time when Emma flew out to visit her son and his family, she rented a condo for a month at a time and decided to stay to help them out. It was going on the second month already. She had thought it would be for just a little while, until he fought off this bad infection in his lungs. But time was going on and on with little light at the end of the tunnel. She watched as her son's life was drifting away and there was nothing anyone could do to help him. They needed a donor who could offer Donnie new lungs. It had been ten months now since he was put on the transplant list. Did it always take this long? She heard horror stories about taking years or patients dying before a donor became available. She prayed that would not happen to her son.

On the way to the hospital, Emma's cell phone rang.

"Hi Liv, I'm so sorry. I over slept, I'm on my way." Emma answered, all flustered.

"Don't rush its okay. I just wanted to let you know that I'm leaving the hospital. I told the babysitter I'd be home by five but the transplant team all came in to talk to Donnie and do some preliminary testing so after asking me a few questions they asked me to leave the room for about half an hour. I just left so take your time."

Olivia was a good wife. She had put up with so much. They were married young and tried for several years to have a child, with no luck. She tried fertility drugs and artificial insemination but still nothing. They contemplated adoption and began looking into it when she learned that she was pregnant, with twins. They are four years old now and just into everything, but Emma loved them with every ounce of her being.

Emma wished her father was still alive to see those kids. He would have adored them. Billy and Beth. And that was their real names; not William and Elizabeth, but Billy Clark and his sister Beth Ann. Towheads, like their mother. With brown eyes like their dad. Just beautiful children. Emma prayed so hard that God wouldn't take their father from them. She dreamed every day that a donor would be found. And she prayed.

Mack died in his sleep on April 17th five years ago. (That is 417 in case you lost count.) He had had a stroke two years prior but he recovered fairly well. Emma talked him into selling the restaurant which took longer than they thought it would, but he finally managed to sell it to his then, head chef. He got a chunk of change up front to put into his bank account, and Mack was financing the rest, for a monthly cash flow. It was working great. And then Mack died suddenly. Those monthly payments now go to Emma, who shares them with her daughters and her son and his family. After all, Donnie has been unable to work for over two years now and those payments come in handy along with his disability payments.

Olivia went back to work when Donnie became disabled and unable to work. He was a stay-at-home dad, but as time wore on the kids had to be put into pre-school when Donnie got seriously ill the previous year. Olivia doesn't make much working at Triple A but its year round work. She has no education or training so she had to take whatever work she could qualify for. She tried waitressing but she was not cut out for the restaurant business and working nights. She did some hostessing for lunch but it didn't pay enough and her schedule changed weekly. She couldn't work around that. She was hired as a receptionist at AAA and then trained to help customers with Trip Tiks. She only works thirty hours a week so they struggle financially. Papa's income helps and Emma is there to pick up the pieces whenever necessary. However the medical bills were mounting. When Donnie was hospitalized and she learned that he was seriously ill, Olivia had to take a leave of absence from her job. The pre-school fees have gone up so she can only afford to put the twins in school three days a week instead of five. Then she needs to rely on babysitters. On top of worrying about Donnie's health, Olivia is stressing over the mounting bills. How will they ever get by without outside help?

Donnie's older sisters help when they can. They've taken turns flying out from Massachusetts to visit Donnie and his family in California a few times. They send money when they can afford a few extra bucks. But Jessie is divorced and went back to school full time since she has no children. She tends bar at night to support herself, along with the monthly allowance Emma sends both of her girls, from Papa's income. And Katie married a wonderful young man who is laid back and has no ambition whatsoever. He is a carpenter who works when the fancy strikes him. He would rather stay home and watch television, play with his three year old son and cook up a mean pot of pasta sauce. Katie is expecting their second child.

Emma got off the elevator on the eighth floor and smiled and spoke to the nurses that she knew now by name. "I'm back" she announced to them.

The transplant team was just leaving Donnie's room when she entered.

"Hi Sweetheart. Any news?"

"No mom. No donor yet. They are just keeping me on track." Donnie was weary and struggling to breathe. He put the oxygen mask back on and closed his eyes. "Sorry Mom, I need to rest." Talking and breathing were taking its toll on his energy. Just breathing alone was burning calories, causing him to lose more weight that he could not afford to lose. He needed to be as strong as he could when the call came for new lungs.

Emma patted his head, pushed the hair away from his face,

kissed his forehead and took her position in her chair. She opened a book to read but instead, her mind once again, began to wander. When you sit by your son's bedside and watch him dying slowly, knowing that you can't do anything to help him but pray, your mind wanders back to those days when it all began.

Chapter 5

1979 - 1980

Emma was alone to raise her two daughters and her son with this incurable disease. She had no one to help her. She had no one to support her. She couldn't work and leave the children with a babysitter because Donnie demanded too much care. She had collected money from Rick's life insurance but it wasn't nearly enough to take care of her for any length of time. She had a mortgage on her house and medical bills that were growing. Dad to the rescue.

"Sell the house and move in with me." Mack told her one day sitting at her kitchen table sharing some seafood stew that he brought to her from his restaurant. He made it himself, fresh that morning.

Her father knew she was struggling. Emma's mother had been a bookkeeper and had taught Emma, so she was doing some bookkeeping jobs from home but it wasn't paying the bills. Donnie was a handful. He was on so much medication and she had to learn how to do his postural drainage therapy which she did four times a day, before each meal and again before bed. She had to equip his crib with a cool-mist tent that constantly needed to be fixed and adjusted. She had to transport him up to Boston every six weeks to be seen by his new doctor, Aubrey Maloney, a brilliant research geneticist. Those appointments lasted all afternoon. Her son had a defective gene that would later be named as a 'Double Delta 508' gene. Donnie was prescribed a special formula to help him put on weight and it smelled like rotten eggs when she prepared it, trying hard not to gag as she did. Emma was drained and the fight was going out of her. She knew her father was right, she needed to sell her house, cut her expenses and live with her father, who could help her from time to time, when he wasn't busy with the deli. Her options were limited. She couldn't depend on friends, they had their own lives.

By the end of spring, Emma found a buyer for her house. She wasn't going to walk away with a lot of money but after she paid off her bills, it would be a nice nest egg for the time being. She could breathe a sigh of relief but she hated leaving the house that she shared with the man she had loved, her husband.

She and Donnie shared a room and the girls had their own

room in the apartment over the deli. Papa's room was at the front of the building while Emma and her children's rooms were in the rear. It was a large apartment.

Emma went to the post office to get a PO Box for her mail since there was no mail delivery to this part of town. Her box number was 714. There they were again, her special numbers. Was it a good omen or not? She had to believe that it was.

Emma had once helped her parents by working in the deli and learning how to do the bookkeeping so she assumed some of the same duties, to help her dad and to pay for her keep. She took over the financial part of the business, relieving the bookkeeper from her job, saving her dad that cost. The bookkeeper was due to have her baby in just a few weeks anyway so the timing was perfect for all concerned. The young girl was once one of Mack's waitresses who helped his wife in the office. When Mack's wife died, she stepped in to do more and more, still waitressing for tips, but when she got married and pregnant, she worried who was going to take over for her. She was so happy when Emma moved in to help her dad. No one realized it had been the other way around; dad was helping Emma.

By the time summer rolled around, when the new season kicked in, Emma was right in the swing of things, working with her father downstairs at the deli and working in the office upstairs in the apartment so she was always near Donnie. Dad was there to watch and help her with Donnie so she could get out on occasion, although she never went far.

Emma found her niche. She began doing bookkeeping jobs for other restaurateurs and small businessmen. She was able to work from her office located in the apartment over the deli, while she could still be close to Donnie and take care of him herself. She had help however. The staff who worked in the deli for her father, adored little Donnie with his pale yellow hair and huge brown eyes. He smiled so easily. He was a happy baby. To look at him, one would never know that he was sickly. The servers took turns babysitting for her and spending time with Donnie and the girls for an hour before or after their shifts. They offered to take Donnie in his carriage for long walks. None of them expected to be paid for their time but Mack always included a bonus in their pay checks each week according to how much time they spent taking care of his grandchildren. Two waitresses became full time babysitters and learned how to do his physical therapy. When they worked in that capacity, Emma paid them herself. She needed to visit with customers and run errands and she needed time alone, at times. Papa too spent time babysitting. He adored his grandchildren and his little family thrived.

She had kept in close contact with her friends Maddie and Bill from Plymouth. Her other friend, Diane, had fallen in love and moved to Texas with a young doctor. She kept in contact via email or phone calls but it wasn't the same as having someone there to go out with and visit.

Every so often Emma would take a day and go back to visit Maddie and her children, with little Donnie, while the girls were in pre-school. Bill had been a huge help to Emma after Rick died, and he spent a lot of time doing things around Emma's house, getting it ready for sale. He was a good guy and a close friend. He loved Rick like a kid brother. He missed him terribly. Emma and Bill formed a bond that is seldom found. She could pick up the phone and call him day or night and she knew that he'd be there for her.

One day when he came home from his twenty four hour shift, he found Emma sitting at his kitchen table with his wife, Maddie, sipping tea and eating butterscotch squares that Emma had baked at home. Donnie was sitting in his little portable jumper seat, jumping up and down and rolling around the kitchen floor. Maddie's kids were outside playing with friends.

"Well if it isn't our favorite Cape Codder." He greeted Emma with a big bear hug.

"And look at this guy jumping all around. He's getting so big, Emma." Bill scooted down to get a better look at smiling Donnie. "He looks great Emma. And so do you. You're wearing your hair differently, right?" Bill stood up and looked directly at Emma. There was a sparkle in his eyes. He had missed her. The attention made her blush.

"I'm here too sweetheart," Maddie stood to give her husband a welcome home kiss. "Want some tea or coffee and a butterscotch square that Emma made?"

He peeled his eyes away from Emma and hugged his wife, excusing himself to go take a quick shower to freshen up. He was tired and wanted to change his clothes.

"You need not pay any attention to him, Emma. After a long shift he gets a little sentimental at times. He sees you and of course, it brings back thoughts of Rick." Maddie was making excuses for her husband, recognizing that Bill made Emma feel uncomfortable. Maddie never had a jealous bone in her body, but still the attention flustered Emma even though she knew Bill adored Maddie.

Emma said she understood and said she needed to be getting back home to pick up the girls from school and to do Donnie's therapy and prepare his food with all the medicine he required. She mixed some crushed pills in applesauce now, before feeding him his meals. He loved his applesauce. She wanted to beat the heavy "after work" traffic going over the Sagamore Bridge, she told Maddie. But they had shared several nice hours together. They hugged good bye and Emma and Donnie were gone by the time Bill came out of the bedroom.

"Did I scare her off?" He asked his wife, reaching for a cold beer. She explained her friend had to leave to take care of her child who required so much attention and care.

"It isn't easy on her, Billy, but she's doing a great job. Moving in with her father was the right thing for her. She is not alone and she gets a lot of help from her father's staff. I miss her. I know you do too, but she's doing well. "

Bill was glad to hear that she was not alone but he still missed seeing her around town and watching the girls and little Donnie grow. When you didn't see them every day, kids tended to grow up so fast.

On her drive home to Dennisport, Emma reflected on her visit. She wondered if her son would ever be able to run around outside and play with other kids like Maddie's children. She wondered if she would ever meet another man and fall in love and have a normal life. What man would ever want her with two girls and a son with an incurable disease that took up so much of her time? With that thought, Emma was ashamed for even thinking like that. She was Donovan's mother and he wouldn't be with her for very long. She would devote her whole life loving him and taking care of him, whatever he needed. God had chosen this life for her. He must have known that she could handle it. There were no answers to the "why me?" question. It was her fate. She needed to face the facts and do her best for her daughters and her son. There was no time for feeling sorry for herself. No pity party time for Emma. "The girls and Donnie are my life," she said out loud, glancing at her sleeping son in his car seat behind her. .

Chapter 6

September 20, 2014

"What were you dreaming about Ma?" Donnie asked as she opened her eyes.

"I was remembering my friends, Maddie and Bill, back in Massachusetts. Do you remember them, Donnie?" Emma smiled. "They were good friends of mine. I haven't thought about them for a long time."

"Of course I remember them" Donnie replied with a thoughtful expression on his face. "I remember the day he came to speak to you alone. You were in your office upstairs over the deli." Donnie paused, taking a few breaths of his oxygen before continuing. "I walked by and your door was open and I saw you hugging him. I thought that was strange, but then I saw you hand him a Kleenex and you grabbed one for yourself. When he pulled away from you, I saw that he was crying. I think that was the first time I ever saw a grown man cry. Other than Papa." He replaced the oxygen, having said too much at once. He breathed as deeply as he could, trying to fill his lungs with air.

"He came to tell me that Maddie was dying of a rare, fast spreading cancer. It was a very sad and emotional day." Emma's eyes filled with tears at the memory.

"I knew enough to leave you two alone so I went downstairs to tell Papa that something was wrong with Bill. I told him you were both crying. Papa made me a Roy Rogers with a cherry and an orange in it, and he sat down with me at a table and we talked like grownups. I miss Papa. He was more like a father than a grandfather to me."

"A Roy Rogers with a cherry and an orange? Donnie you remember the darndest things sometimes." Emma laughed.

"After Billy left that day I began thinking about Maddie and all the pieces started to fit. Being a nurse, she suspected something was seriously wrong long before she was diagnosed and even then, she kept it a secret. There was no cure; and no treatment that was going to make much difference." Emma reflected on those days, so long ago, when her friend was dying much too soon.

"Mom, remember her Thanksgiving dinner?" Donnie smiled with the memory.

"You have such a memory, Donnie. The details you recall are uncanny. Yes, of course I remember." And Emma gave a little chuckle. It was a great memory.

"Maddie called me one day out of the blue. She had been doing that quite often, as a matter of fact. She just wanted to talk. That day she told me she missed me and wished we lived closer. She invited us to Sunday dinner. She said she was craving a nice turkey dinner with all the fixings. I laughed and told her it wasn't quite time for Thanksgiving yet and she laughed. She knew. She knew she wouldn't make it 'til then."

Emma paused, thinking about that day. "So you and I and the girls drove up to her house around noon time, so I could help. Bill had been working for twenty four hours and was due home mid-afternoon, so she planned to eat around three o'clock. When he came in the door, the smells of turkey and stuffin' hit him in the face. I'll never forget what he said." Emma paused with recollection, wanting to repeat it correctly, but Donnie beat her to it.

"He said 'I went to work in September and came home on

Thanksgiving. How in the world did that happen?' and everyone laughed." Donnie stole breaths of oxygen before going on.

"I remember how Maddie laughed at me when I asked for more mashed potatoes and peas. Everyone else was stuffed but they were my favorite foods. Still are, now that I think about it." He smiled as he breathed through his plastic mask.

"Oh Donnie, that was such a nice day, but I do remember how exhausted Maddie was by the end of the day. Bill's mother and I insisted she go lie down while we cleaned up but she wanted to package up the left overs. She cooked enough for an army. What she was doing was freezing the dinner so her family would have it on Thanksgiving. She died two weeks before the holiday."

"You and Bill stayed friends for a long time, didn't you? You used to take me, Jess and Katie and he would take his kids and we'd go places together, like when we went to the zoo. Remember? He'd bring his kids down to the Cape and we'd spend the day at the beach with him. His kids were older than us but they were fun. I liked being with them. It was like being part of a bigger family."

Emma just bowed her head with the memory. It was so good to share fond memories like this with her son. She tried to give him some happy times when she could.

"Ma, what happened to him? He stopped coming around one day and you never mentioned him again. Did you guys have a fight?"

"Life gets in the way sometimes, Donnie. He had his job as a fireman in Plymouth and his kids needed him since they no longer had a mother, even though their grandmother lived with them. I had you kids and I had to help Papa at the Deli and I had my little odd jobs. We lived quite a distance away from them, and…" her voice trailed off for a minute in retrospect. Realizing that her son was now an adult, she thought he deserved to hear the whole truth.

"Billy and I started to get too close, Donnie. I didn't feel it could work out. There were too many ghosts, too many memories we each clinged to. Your father was his best friend and we both missed him so talked often about him and that kept an old wound open and sore. And of course Maddie was my dear friend and again, we both missed her. We were always talking about times that were in the past.

We needed to move on. I told him that we shouldn't see each other anymore, Donnie. It was about three years after Maddie died and he was looking for a relationship; a mother for his kids. I just couldn't step into that role for him. It was better if we just cut the rope and parted as friends. We still keep in touch with an occasional email or birthday card. He never did re-marry."

"Neither did you."

"No, Donnie, I didn't. You kids were my whole life. You were all I needed, the three of you and Papa." Emma smiled at her son with loving eyes. "And now there's Liv and Beth and little Billy and Katie's Charlie. My life is full." She didn't want to think about the fact that since Donnie was fourteen, she kept wondering how much longer he had to live. She had no idea where that time had gone but she was grateful for having it.

Emma closed her eyes and said a silent prayer: *please don't take him from me now, dear Lord. He is still needed here. Please send a donor.*

When she opened her eyes, Donnie had fallen back to sleep,

exhausted.

She sat back in the chair and closed her eyes once again and thought back to the days when Maddie was gone and Billy reached out to Emma.

Emma always kept busy between taking care of her son and the girls and her father and doing her jobs, taking care of bookkeeping for so many small businessmen who didn't have a clue about paperwork. She was always taking care of other people and Bill slipped right into that niche. He was a single parent, like Emma. His mother lived in his house and helped care for his kids but it wasn't the same for him as having a woman to talk to, to confide in, and to kiss good night.

Emma had been on her own and alone for many years by the time Maddie died. She had gone out on dates here and there but her world wasn't ready to take on another person to take care of. A steady relationship would only complicate her already complicated life. But Bill was different from other men. He was a friend. He was her husband's best friend and her best friend's husband. They shared so many good times together before Maddie died. He was lonely and unprepared to be a single parent. Emma was there to fill the void and show him the ropes. She suggested that they take their children on picnics and whale watches and one weekend they went up into the mountains of New Hampshire where they rented a large cabin. It was on the third anniversary of Maddie's death and Emma thought it would be good to get his kids out of town and keep them busy.

They rented bicycles and went hiking through the woods on trails marked on the visitor's map. One night they built a campfire after dark and toasted marshmallows to make smores. It was their last night at the cabin. The kids were all in bed sound asleep. Emma and Bill sat out on the deck sipping wine and listening to the crickets and the noises of the night in the woods.

They sat in silence for several minutes just enjoying the peace and quiet when Bill broke the silence.

"I love you; ya know that, don't ya, Emma?" He reached over and held her hand.

"I know Billy boy. I love you too. But," she began to say all the things she had said before, to halt what she knew would come next, but Bill caught her off guard and kissed her before she could say another word.

She let him. She even kissed him back. He stood up and pulled her up and into his arms and kissed her again, hard and passionately. It felt so good to be in his arms. It felt natural and it felt good. She too had been lonely for a long time. She did love him. But was it enough?

"No, Bill. No. Please, no." She pushed herself away. "I do love you, but it can never work. You know that. We've discussed it before. We each have our own lives, our own children. I've got my dad, you have your mom. It just won't work, Billy. I'm so sorry."

Emma picked up her glass of wine and went into the house. She poured the wine down the drain and put the glass in the sink. Bill followed her inside and put his hands on her shoulders, stepping up behind her.

"Don't walk away from me, Emma. Please. We can make it work. I know we can." He spun her around to see the tears as they spilled from her eyes. He kissed her again, then held her in his arms, never wanting to let go, for fear that he'd never get her back.

Bill's youngest son opened the bedroom door, rubbing his eyes.

"I need to pee, Dad." He explained, walking into the bathroom.

Emma pulled away from Bill's embrace, not wanting the children to see them like that. They would never understand. Emma was Mom's friend. How could she be in Dad's embrace? It just wasn't right for the children, Emma reminded Bill all too often.

Bill walked his son back to bed and tucked him in. Emma used the bathroom then escaped into the room she was sharing with her kids. She made sure the blankets were covering them and she climbed into her own small bed by the window. But sleep did not come easily. She had a decision to make and by morning, she had decided to tell Bill they wouldn't be seeing each other anymore. It was one of the hardest things she ever had to do but it was the only way. Her heart was already breaking. She did it for the children.

Chapter 7

September 20 - 21, 2014

Emma sat there in the chair with her eyes closed, resting, listening to the never ending hospital noises; nurses talking out in the hallway and the constant droning of the machines that were keeping her son alive.

Emma opened her eyes and sat up in her chair, looking at her son.

"Did you say something, Donnie? Sorry dear, I didn't hear you."

Donnie lifted the mask that partially covered his face, enabling him to breathe.

"I said," he chuckled, having forgotten that people couldn't understand his mumbling behind the plastic mask. "I liked him. Billy. He was cool, Mom. I missed him when you stopped seeing him. I don't think I ever told you that."

"No, Donnie, you never did. He was a great man. I missed him too, but I just couldn't figure out how we could ever make things work. He deserved a chance to get on with his life and find a woman to help him with his children. I was not that person, Donnie"

"But what about you, Mom? You deserved a chance at life too!" Donnie felt badly for his mother giving up her life to take care of him. "Papa didn't need taking care of. He did fine until we moved in with him. He would've been okay if we left."

"I had a life, Donnie. Taking care of you kids and Papa. That was my life. That's enough for me, Donnie. I love you." Emma's guilt over being a part of the cause for her son's disease, kept her in check. Nothing would keep her from doing her very best to care for her son.

Emma was sincere and honest however, when Donnie left home to get married, there was a big void in Emma's life; emptiness that she just never could fill. All three of her children moved away and she was left at the deli with just her father to look after. She did get lonely often back then.

Donnie cleared his throat and brought Emma back to the present.

"I named my son after him, Ma. I never told you that either.

And Beth was named after Olivia's grandmother. They are two people who were important in our lives."

Emma was surprised. She did not know that but she was getting uncomfortable with this discussion. She didn't want her son to feel bad or think he had ruined her life. She needed to change the subject, but just then a nurse came in to check Donnie's sugar levels and to give him insulin if needed.

"I'm going to go get a cup of coffee, Donnie. I'll be back in a few minutes," Emma told her son, knowing the nurse would be occupying his time for a little while.

Emma rode down in the elevator from the eighth floor and walked to the cafeteria where they had the worst food on earth. Most of the patients in this hospital had a serious illness and they needed to be strong for surgery when it became available and yet somehow the food was almost un-edible. Emma often came down to the cafeteria to buy something packaged to bring back to Donovan to supplement the food that was served to him, which he couldn't eat. How did they mess up scrambled eggs or a grilled cheese sandwich? So Emma took her time and looked around for something she thought her son would like to eat; something filling but low in sugar and carbohydrates.

When Donnie was first diagnosed, patients with Cystic Fibrosis rarely lived into the adult stages but now with new medicines and treatments, these patients were living into their thirties and forties. A new dilemma however, many were developing Diabetes which was onset by CF. As a child, having no digestive enzymes, Donnie had to stay away from any fried or fatty foods. He couldn't have McDonald's french fries or peanut butter and jelly like other kids. No grilled cheese sandwiches or even whole milk or milkshakes. Donnie chose to fill up on cereal and potatoes and pasta dishes, all of which were "carbs". Now all these years later, he can no longer have those foods, and that made gaining weight an even bigger challenge. So what do you feed someone who cannot eat fats OR carbohydrates? Emma looked around the self serve cafeteria.

They had a "make your own omelet" station so she put some peppers and onions and diced up ham into the scrambled egg mixture and poured it into the omelet pan. She grabbed some packets of ketchup and napkins and grabbed a Danish for herself with a cup of coffee. She paid for her food and went back upstairs where Donnie was resting and gazing out his hospital window. There wasn't much to see from the eighth floor. He wished he was strong enough to get up to go out for some fresh air.

Mom put the foods down on his hospital tray and used the electric remote to raise his bed up a bit higher.

"I made you a western omelet, Donnie. Hope that will tickle your fancy." She said as she pulled the Styrofoam container from the paper bag.

"Smells good. You should have seen what they served for dinner, Mom. I have no idea what it was supposed to be but it tasted like garbage."

Emma smiled. He said that about every meal. She refilled his water cup and pulled her chair over closer to the bed to eat with her son.

"We are having breakfast at eight o'clock at night. It will probably raise my sugars but I didn't get much from my dinner tray other than the weak soup and the sugar free Jell-O."

"Good thing the nurse already checked your sugars, but this is all healthy and good for you; low carbs, Donnie."

"It's great Mom. You should open a restaurant. You're a good cook." It was their standard inside joke, since she worked with her father in the kitchen of his deli all those years. Emma smiled and shook her head.

"I was going to get you something else to drink but I know you don't drink soda and you rarely have milk other than in cereal. Do you want me to go get you a cup of tea? They have cups and hot water at the nurses' kitchenette. You have your own tea here, right?"

Donnie lit up. He enjoyed tea with honey. So once Emma finished her Danish she went to fetch him a cup of his antioxidant tea, which would also help him sleep. She returned and he had his tea while she finished her strong black coffee. They talked a while and he got a little teary eyed when he spoke of his children and how he missed them. And at that point, Emma could see him struggling to breathe. She checked his oxygen levels on the monitor and told him to sit back and rest. She lowered the back of his bed and she put the television on low. He was asleep in minutes. He was always a good sleeper, as long as his belly was full. Patients with CF need at least ten hours of sleep a night and Donnie was no exception. Now he slept almost double that, having no energy at all. Even in his sleep, he burned calories trying to breathe. Emma turned down the lights and covered him up. No matter how old your child gets, he's still your little boy. She sat back in her chair, slipped her feet out of her shoes and put her feet up on the end of the reclining chair and she watched a few programs on TV until her eyes got heavy, then she closed them and drifted off to sleep.

Emma woke a few hours later and quietly got up and slipped out of her son's room to take a short walk up the hallway, stretch her legs. All was quiet except the few night nurses chatting with one another. She used the public rest room while she was out and about.

When Emma returned, Donnie was sitting up, coughing and coughing, and unable to stop nor to catch his breath. Emma ran to the nurse's station and asked for help. Two nurses came running. By the time they entered his room and turned on the light, Donnie was hanging his head over the side of the bed. The coughing had almost stopped but blood was pouring from his nose and throat.

Emma gasped and held her breath, standing back, away from his bed to let the nurses take care of him. With all the times that Emma had witnessed this occurrence, she still could not get used to seeing her son in this situation. It brought tears to her eyes. The membranes in his throat break down from the constant heavy coughing.

The nurses on this floor knew their job and they took such good care of her son. They were to be commended. They soothed him and calmed him and then proceeded to work as a team to change him and his bedding, discarding the bloody sheets. They gave him some ice chips to suck on to help soothe his raw throat.

"Are you okay now there, young man? Anything I can get for you?" One of the nurses stood by his bedside while the other nurse refilled his pitcher with fresh cold water.

Donnie, weak from the ordeal, gasping to get the oxygen back into his damaged lungs, just shook his head. One nurse put a cold, wet facecloth on his forehead to help fight off the headache she knew he would have. She patted Emma on the forearm as she left mother and son to be alone once again. She shut off the bright overhead lights on her way out of the room.

Emma stood beside his bed and held her son's hand. She kissed his cheek, closed her eyes and asked God to please hurry up and send him a donor.

They both had a rough night. Donnie was restless and unable to sleep much. Emma tried to help him get more comfortable but she was beginning to annoy him and she backed off and sat back down in her chair.

"Let me know if I can do anything for you, Don." Her voice was barely louder than a whisper.

"Fine, Ma. Fine. Just leave me alone for now, okay. Thanks." Donnie was agitated. He was so tired of being sick and tired all of the time. Some days he was ready to give up the fight, but he knew he could never do that. His wife and kids loved him, along with his mother, who had devoted her life to him. He could never stop fighting.

He just wanted to get well and go home. He wanted to see his children and play daddy again.

When he drifted off to sleep, Emma sent his wife a text message: "Hard night. If possible, can you bring in the kids tomorrow morning and I'll take them home with me. He is missing all of you right now."

Children coming in to visit on the eighth floor was not a recommended practice but on occasion they made exceptions. The kids had to be dressed in masks and gowns and plastic gloves and they could not stay long, but Emma felt it was time. Donnie had not seen his children in almost three weeks. Skype was nice, but not the same as seeing them in person.

Emma was surprised when Olivia texted her right back. It was long after midnight. She should have been asleep. But it was hard on her too. She added that Billy had a nightmare and she just got him back to sleep, so visiting their dad was a good idea.

Chapter 8

Olivia woke up in the morning to the children running around and screaming. Billy was chasing Beth because she had taken his stuffed dog off his bed. Even though he was four years old, Billy still slept with the animal his dad had given him for Christmas a year ago. Donnie told his son that he'd have to learn to take good care of the stuffed dog before he could have a real dog and Billy never forgot that. He was screaming at his sister to give it back to him.

Olivia dragged her weary bones out of bed, slipped her feet into her slippers and went to investigate what all the commotion was about. Beth was hugging the doggie and giggling, playing keep away. Billy took one look at his mother and cried.

"Make her give it back, Mommy. It's mine. Daddy gave it to me to take care of. She's going to mess it up." Big crocodile tears ran down his cheeks.

"Beth Ann, give your brother back his toy, now, please."

"It's not a toy, Mom, it's my Buddy," Billy cried.

"Beth, give Buddy back to Billy. Be a good girl. I have a

surprise for both of you but you have to stop screaming and be good children."

Beth handed the stuffed dog to her brother and asked what the surprise was.

"First I want you to come into the kitchen and we'll all have a nice breakfast then I'll tell you about the surprise." Olivia led the way, down the stairs and into the kitchen where she gave them each some orange juice and prepared their breakfast.

"Yum, blueberry pancakes," said Billy, sitting up big and tall after finishing his juice.

"I don't like blueberries," Beth pouted.

"I know, darling. I am going to put some peaches in your pancakes." Beth smiled.

As the children ate quietly, Olivia sipped her second cup of coffee and picked at the pancakes on her plate; one blueberry and one peach, so both children would be happy.

"What is our surprise, Mommy?" Beth asked as she took her last bite, syrup running down her chin.

"Wipe your mouth with your napkin, Beth. Well I talked to your daddy last night and he said that he really misses you guys. So instead of going to day care today, I am going to take you into the hospital to visit with daddy for a little while." She smiled.

The kids started clapping and jumping up and down in their seats. They were all excited.

"You have to be good kids though and watch your manners and talk softly. Remember daddy is very sick so you can't jump all over him. You need to be gentle. Can you do that?" They both agreed in unison.

"Okay, let's go upstairs and wash up and brush our teeth and I'll pick out some nice clothes for you to wear, okay?" The kids raced up the stairs and into the bathroom.

The telephone rang before Olivia made it to the top of the stairs. She turned around and walked back down four steps, reaching over the banister, she picked up the house phone. "Hello."

"Hi. Mrs. Clark?" the voice on the phone inquired. "This is Maria from Burbank Water and Power. This is a courtesy call to let you know that if your bill is not paid in three days, they will be turning off your electricity." The woman went on to tell her what she had to do and what it would cost her if she had the power turned off and how much it would cost to have it restarted.

Olivia thanked her and closed her eyes as she hung up the phone. The bills were just piling up. Donnie had always taken care of the finances and with him being sick in the hospital, it was just one more thing for Olivia to take care of. The stress was mounting. They had fifteen dollars in their checking account and the savings was almost depleted. She would have to ask her mother in law for help, without Donnie knowing it. It was something she dreaded but she didn't want him to worry about it. He needed to stay strong and be ready when the call came for new lungs. How was she ever going to get through this? She just wanted to sit down and cry but she had to be strong.

Olivia went to the desk they had set up in the corner of the dining area and looked at the pile of bills. Sure enough, two months of electric bills were still sitting there unpaid. She sat down at the computer and went online to check her bank balance and to see when the last payment was made for the power company. Donnie had made a partial payment three days before he went into the hospital, over three weeks prior.

"Mommy, where are my clothes?" Beth yelled from the top of the stairs.

"I'm coming honey," Olivia said wearily, on the verge of tears.

She closed the laptop and dragged herself up the stairs to pick out the clothes for her children. Then she slipped into the shower to get ready to go see her dying husband.

Olivia parked the car in the hospital garage and before leaving the car, she once again informed the children how they needed to behave. She told them that Nana would take them home with her when she left and Mommy would be home later. They said they understood. So they all held hands and walked quietly into the hospital entrance and took the elevator up to the eighth floor.

People always looked at Olivia when she was with her two

children. They were a beautiful family. Liv was only about five foot three and she wore a size one. She wore her platinum blond hair down to her shoulders, tucked behind her ear on one side. She had the bluest eyes and fairest skin that Donnie had ever seen. She was strikingly beautiful and her white-blond children with their contrasting brown eyes complimented her beauty. The people in the elevator smiled and said hello to the well behaved children.

Emma was helping Donnie into the chair to be more accessible to greet his children. Liv had called his cell when they were entering the lobby. Donnie had his mother help him wash up and comb his ash colored hair and it just about did him in. He was sitting there, taking deep breaths of oxygen so he could remove the mask and just use the nose cannula or prongs in the nose, so he could talk to his kids and give them kisses through his blue paper mask.

Olivia stopped at the nurses' station and they were taken to a store room where the children were given masks to put over their mouths and they put paper gowns over their clothes. They thought it was a game. They giggled and laughed. The nurse cut off some of it so the children would not trip when they walked. She led them to see their father.

"Daddy, Daddy," they squealed with delight. They forgot to go easy and be quiet. They were so happy to finally see their father. Hugs and kisses galore. Beth jumped up to sit on her father's lap.

Then Billy's eyes got wide as he looked around to see all the machines that were connected to his father.

"Daddy, are you going to die?" Billy was pale and visibly afraid.

Olivia grabbed him by his shoulders and pulled him into her arms, stooping down to his level. She hugged him tight.

"Daddy is just waiting to get new lungs. He is not going to die, Billy. We need to keep praying to God to find him new lungs soon." How do you explain to a four year old that someone else needed to die in order for his father to live?

A nurse entered the room to take Donnie's vitals and the kids wanted to know what she was doing. She had children of her own so she was very understanding and was letting them listen to their hearts through the stethoscope and she was showing them what she was going to do to their father.

Olivia took that moment to ask Emma to step outside for a minute. She had to tell her about the electric bill. She was all choked up with tears in her eyes.

"Where is the bill, Liv?" Emma asked, trying to comfort her.

Olivia told her where to find the bill on the desk. Emma said she'd take care of it while she had the kids for the day. She told Olivia not to worry.

"Please, don't upset yourself. Come to me anytime when you need help. That's why I am here, Olivia. I'll take care of it." She pulled her daughter in law into an embrace and kissed her cheek.

When it was time to leave, the nurse told the children they could keep the mask and gown to play at home but she helped them remove them and wrap them up. She put it all into a plastic bag for them to take with them when they left with Nana.

Emma took them to their own house first, so they could change into play clothes and have some lunch. She looked through the cabinets and in the fridge but there was very little food to eat. She found the pile of bills on the desk. She told the kids she would take them out to lunch if they would just go watch television for a few minutes until she could do some work for Mommy.

Emma sat down at the desk and looked at the bills that needed to be paid right away. The cell phone bill was due three days ago. To be on a transplant list it was mandatory to have an active cell phone along with a home phone. In case one was inoperable, they needed to be able to contact the patient It was mandatory. Emma wrote out a check for the cell phone bill and put it into the respective envelope. She put the electric bill aside and continued to look at the other bills. The credit card bill was there and Emma, not wanting to pry, but curious to see what Olivia had been charging, she went through the bill item by item. The poor girl was using her credit card for food and gas for the car. Not much else. Emma wrote out a check for that and put it with the stub into its envelope, four hundred and twenty three dollars, two months worth of purchases. The last payment had been made almost four weeks ago in the amount of thirty dollars, the bare

minimum due. Emma sighed. How are these kids going to survive, she

wondered. Emma was glad to be of help but she couldn't support them

forever. She found several bills for medical supplies and medications

but she needed to discuss those bills with Olivia. They had to have

some kind of medical assistance on top of the secondary insurance.

She was sure they had to be getting some financial help, but she didn't

know from whom. She found some stamps…she would mail the bills

on their way out, on their way to the power company where she would

pay the bill in full for the two months, so that the electricity would not

be turned off. She didn't want to chance mailing a check in case it

wouldn't get posted in time to their account. The last thing Olivia

needed was to have her power turned off. As she was about to put the

remaining bills away, she noticed an overdue notice from the landlord,

looking for a rent payment. "Oh dear Lord," Emma said out loud. She

looked at the notice. The rent was due on the first of the month. They

had a ten day grace period, but today was the twenty first of the

month. She'd have to discuss this with her daughter in law. Emma was paying for a small condo nearby so she could be of help but she also had her house back in Massachusetts. She had closed it up for a few months and had someone watching it for her, but her bills still continued. She had to leave the heat on so her pipes wouldn't freeze.

No wonder Olivia was stressed, Emma thought, feeling the anxiety herself. Donnie's disability check was due to come in on the fourth Thursday of the month. That would go for the rent. But then a week later, another month's rent would be due. There was very little light at the end of the financial tunnel for her son and his family. He needed to get new lungs so he could get well and get back on his feet and help support them once again. But even after having the surgery, rehabilitation would be an ongoing thing for many months. Emma closed her eyes, trying not to shed a tear, worrying about her son.

"What's the matter, Nana?" Beth asked when she saw her sitting there with her eyes closed. "When are we going to lunch? I'm hungry." With that, Billy came over and said that he was hungry too. Emma smiled and stood up, leaving the notice on the desk.

She took the kids to McDonald's for lunch and bought them

Happy Meals. Then they went to the office of the power company and she paid that bill. From there she took the kids to the grocery store and bought about two hundred dollars worth of groceries. She took the children back to their house and put the groceries away and then gave them each a dish of ice cream that she bought for them. Then all three of them went upstairs and turned on the TV in their parents' bedroom and lied down together on Mommy's big bed and took a nap. That's where Liv found them when she came home at four o'clock.

Chapter 9

"Oh, you're home early," Emma said when she opened her eyes to see Olivia standing there watching her children sleep.

"Yeah, they had to take Donnie downstairs for some tests so I left. He'll be busy for a good hour or two they told me. I was just about to climb into bed with you guys," she teased as she tickled her little girl and pulled her into a big hug. She reached over and messed Billy's hair.

"Whatcha do all day, kids? Did you wear Nana out?" Olivia was sitting on the edge of her bed while Emma stood up, and brushed her wrinkled clothes.

"No, Momma, Nana wore US out," Beth said laughing, looking at her grandmother. "We had fun. We went to McDonald's for lunch."

"And Nana bought us some ice cream when we went shopping." Billy added.

Olivia looked at Emma, somewhat embarrassed, knowing there was so little food in the house.

"Thank you, Emma. The kids haven't had ice cream in a very

long time. I'm sure it was a treat they enjoyed."

The kids ran off to play downstairs and Olivia turned the television off with the remote that was on the table beside the bed.

"Liv," Emma began. "We need to talk about the bills. I paid the electric bill in person. I didn't want to chance having the check get lost in the mail. And I paid your cell phone bill and your credit card bill. But what about the medical bills? And the overdue rent?"

After dealing with her daughter in law's break down, crying hysterically, Emma went home to her rented condo about ten minutes away. She was exhausted but she made herself a cup of tea and made some phone calls, and did some online research. She set up a Donation website for her son and his family. She couldn't absorb their finances alone. They needed help. She then hopped into a hot shower and put on some comfortable clothes to go back to the hospital to spend the night in the chair next to her son's bed.

Emma had picked up a small rotisserie chicken at the super market along with some three bean salad and she brought that into the hospital with her so she and Donnie could have dinner together, something other than awful hospital food. She had grabbed some paper plates and utensils from home and took them along with her.

While they sat there eating, watching television, playing along with Wheel of Fortune, Emma's cell phone rang. Normally she had her phone turned off but she had forgotten to shut it down.

"Hello." She didn't recognize the caller ID phone number but she knew the area code. It was from her part of Massachusetts.

"Emma? Is that you?" The voice was strong and deep and Emma knew it immediately. She held her breath in surprise.

"Yes, Bill. It's me." She couldn't believe that he would call her after all these years.

"I can't believe you still have the same number. I wasn't sure so I just took a chance. Listen, Emma," Bill was shocked he was actually able to contact her on the first try.

"I just happened to go on Face Book and saw that donation post you have on there. My son got me to finally "get with it" and join Face Book and there you were. It was like a shock. Why didn't I do this sooner? But when I saw it, I just had to call to talk to you and find out how Donnie is doing. Where are you Emma?" Bill couldn't talk fast enough. He just blurted it all out and then took a deep breath.

"Actually Bill, I am sitting beside Donnie right now, in his hospital room." Emma was reluctant to go into details about how seriously ill her son was, while sitting beside him. She smiled at Donnie and stood up and walked out of the room to talk privately.

"But, Emma, WHERE are you? WHAT hospital? In Boston?" Bill was anxious to know all the details.

"No Bill. Donnie and his family moved to Burbank California about two years ago to be near this hospital that specializes in transplants and takes care of adults with Cystic Fibrosis. It's a great place. He's very ill, Billy. As I posted, he needs new lungs."

"His family, you said? Donnie is married with a family?" Bill was shocked. It was hard to believe that Donnie had grown up and was well enough to have a family of his own. "That's great. I'm so happy for him. And for you?"

"The hospital is in Los Angeles, Bill, so that's where we are now. His wife is home with their two children. They are twins, age four," she explained briefly.

"Emma." Bill paused. "I too am in Los Angeles right now. My son lives out here, too. I came to visit him just a few days ago. I'm only here for a week. I would love to see you and Donnie. Can he have visitors?"

Emma's heart skipped a beat. She hadn't seen Bill in more than seven years, when they met up at a party given for charity by the fire department. They both had dates with them on that evening so there was not much discussion but it took Emma weeks to stop thinking about him again. Little did she know, Bill picked up the phone and started to call her on many occasions. He still had strong feelings for her. But he figured she was probably married to the man who accompanied her to the party.

Emma now explained that Donnie was susceptible to infection and germs and he was waiting for a donor. He couldn't have visitors other than family. Bill asked if she'd meet him for coffee or for lunch the next day. Emma hesitated. She hadn't had much sleep and she would be exhausted when she left Donnie in the morning. She would need to get some rest.

"How about if we meet for a late lunch or early dinner. I usually come in to see Donnie around five and spend the night here, so I sleep during the day. On and off. Why not meet me for a bite to eat around three tomorrow? Will that work for you?" Emma's heart was pounding. Was she making a mistake? It was just lunch. He was going back home next week. What harm could it do? He suggested a place not far from the hospital, right off the highway. She agreed to see him then.

She returned to Donnie's room and she looked like the cat that ate the canary.

"So what's up? What was that all about, Mom?" Donnie questioned her.

Emma told him about the website she created and saw him cringe.

"I know you don't want to ask for help, Donnie, but the stress of the mounting bills is getting to Olivia. I love you dearly but I can't support your family, Donnie. I'll do what I can to help but we need outside help. Please understand. People realize that you are very sick and can't work. The holidays are coming. Olivia needs money, Donnie."

Emma explained that she posted the website on Face Book and hoped that some of her friends would make donations to help her son and his family. She had to tell him even though he felt embarrassed at having to ask for help. It was time for him to swallow his pride. He no longer could work to support his family. His disability checks weren't nearly enough to sustain a family of four. The monthly payments from Papa's deli weren't big enough to offset the difference in his expenses. Emma had been using her own share of that income to help them but it still wasn't enough.

"I haven't told Livvy about it yet. I thought I'd see how it worked first. I don't want to get her hopes up for nothing."

Donnie didn't like the idea that his mother did that without consulting him first, but in his heart he knew she did the right thing. Olivia was never very good with budgets and paying the bills but he had been too ill to ask her about finances. So he asked Emma.

"How bad is it? Has she paid any bills at all since I've been here?" Now Donnie had to face what he was trying to avoid.

Emma told him what she had done and said other than the medical bills and the rent, everything was paid up to date. She tried to comfort him.

"Mom. Thanks. I don't know what we'd do without you. You come out here, rent a place to be nearby us and you buy us food and pay our bills. I'm so sorry Mom." Donnie's eyes flooded with tears. He was ashamed.

"Donnie, there is no need to thank me. You and the girls are my whole life. I will do anything for you, you know that. But I'm a realist. I can't do it all. Don't worry about it. We'll figure something out, honey." The last thing she wanted to do was to stress him out.

"And please, don't be sorry. It's not your fault that you have this disease. If your father and I were not both carriers of the defective gene, then you'd be healthy. It is I who must say I'm sorry. I've carried that guilt all of your life. I'm so sorry, Donnie. Dad and I passed this dreadful disease onto you." She reached over and hugged her son as tears ran down her cheeks.

Donnie got very quiet and soon he drifted off to sleep. Emma cleaned up around him, got him some fresh water and wiped down the hospital tray table. She then turned the lights down low and assumed her position in her recliner chair. She texted messages to both of her daughters to give them updates on their brother's condition. "Failing."

A nurse came in a few minutes later and offered Emma a pillow and a blanket to put over her. Emma accepted both and kicked off her shoes and closed her eyes when the nurse left the room. She drifted off to sleep with thoughts of seeing Bill the next day.

Emma's dreams took her back in time to when her father's health had been failing and Emma observed that he was slowing down; no longer able to do what he used to do. The stroke had left him weak on the right side and zapped him of the endless energy that he always had.

Emma had talked her father into putting the deli up for sale in

2008. She knew that it was time for her to start thinking about where she was going to go once the place sold. Her father told her that he'd give her a down payment on a house as payment for all the work she had done for him over the years. He explained that once he was gone she was going to end up with it anyway. She agreed to his offer but only if he agreed to move in with her, where ever she went. It was a pact. Her dad knew his time was short.

Emma found an adorable winterized cottage right across the street from a private beach. It was small and only had two bedrooms and a small den which she converted into an office. With both of her girls and Donnie being married and living on their own, it was all she needed for her and her father. It had a lovely front porch with jalousie windows that could be opened in spring and summer to let the fresh air in through the screens and closed up in the colder months. It had a pellet stove out there so the porch could be used year round. Emma loved the cottage and spent her days painting and decorating before she moved in. She went to flea markets and garage sales and thrift stores looking for just the right furnishings. Some of her father's furniture would work but she didn't want that. She wanted this to be her very own place; one that she could share with her dad. She had sold her own house furnished except for a few personal belongings.

Emma would take long walks along the sands of the beach and sit for hours out on her porch people watching. One day while on a walk, barefoot in the wet sand, she met a man who was helping a little boy with his kite. She assumed it was his son but after talking for a while, Emma learned that the child was his nephew. The man was a little taller than average, sandy blonde hair and dark eyes. Emma realized that she must have been drawn to him because he reminded her of her own son, only older. They had the same coloring and build but Jack was more muscular. He was very easy to talk to. After their lengthy conversation, she deducted that the man was a big shot property developer and he was probably very wealthy. His nephew seemed to adore him but wanted more of his attention so Jack invited Emma to meet him for a drink later that afternoon so they could get to know each other a little better.

He was a few years younger than Emma but it didn't seem to

matter. They had dated a few times when he invited her to go with him to a charity affair in Hyannis, in the mid-cape area. He told her that he did a lot with different charities and this was a fund raiser for a family whose house had burned to the ground. He was donating funds to help rebuild the house. Since Emma had a soft spot for fires and firemen, she agreed to go. It was there, at that fund raiser, where she ran into Bill.

Her date, Jack Hynes, was off talking to some people and Emma was sitting at a table with some people she had never met before. They were making small talk when she looked across the room and saw *him.* She gasped out loud, causing the woman next to her to look in Bill's direction and ask if Emma was all right.

She excused herself, heading in Bill's direction when she noticed the young blonde woman on the other side of him. Emma stopped dead in her tracks. Well of course, he'd be with a woman. Did she think he'd be waiting around for her all these years? Suddenly she felt stupid and was about to make an about face, when Bill spotted her. He never hesitated but came right over to say hello, leaving his date to stand alone.

Emma had taken pride in her makeup and her hair style that night. Jack was well known all over Cape Cod and she wanted to make a good impression. She had even bought a new dress for the occasion. So she was looking good and she knew it.

"Emma," he had said in greeting her. He took her hands in his and pulled her closer to kiss her cheek. Emma blushed and her heart pounded madly.

"Hi Billy. What brings you to Cape Cod?" He was the last person she ever expected to see at this function.

Billy explained that the house that burned down belonged to the sister of one of the firemen he worked with. All the guys who weren't working were expected to make a showing. He told her she might recognize a few faces but they had a lot of new recruits.

God, he looked good, Emma thought. He had a few laugh lines in the corners of his eyes and he was graying at the temples but it only gave him character. He was still in great shape, no pot belly. He was so handsome. He smiled so easily. She missed him terribly. Her heart was aching.

"Oh there you are," Jack walked up beside her. "Hello there. I'm Jack Hynes," he introduced himself to Bill. They shook hands and exchanged pleasantries then Bill excused himself to go back to the blonde lady who never took her eyes off of him or off Emma.

Emma kept looking in the direction to where Bill disappeared but she never saw him again all night. She danced a few dances with Jack and was introduced to so many people she was exhausted from smiling. Everyone either hugged or kissed her and it was becoming annoying to Emma. She just wanted to go home and was very happy when Jack suggested they bow out early.

They stopped for a night cap on the way home and Jack told Emma she was the most beautiful woman at the function. She smiled sweetly thinking Jack was getting a little buzzed. He then invited her to go away with him for the weekend. He was going to take his nephew camping up in Maine. His sister was going through a divorce and Jack was trying to step in to help her with his nephew. He told Emma that he had been married for six years but never had any children of his own. He loved kids but his wife had a modeling career and wouldn't think of giving it up to have children, so they divorced.

As tempting as Jack made it sound, Emma declined the offer stating that she didn't want to interfere. She knew his nephew needed his alone time with Uncle Jack.

"And besides that, I need to help my father. He is selling his Deli Restaurant. There was an offer on the table, to purchase it. I need to begin packing up his things and help him clean out the storage areas." There was no big rush but it was a good excuse not to go with Jack and his nephew. There would be other times for them to get away.

The days and weeks that followed were thoughts of Billy. She longed to see him again. But he had a woman in his life. Maybe they could just be friends? No. He had suggested that when she broke it off with him and she knew, as well as he did, that it would never work. They were too involved to be "just" friends. Eventually Emma got so busy packing up her father's belongings that thoughts of Bill just faded once again.

Emma dated Jack on and off but he was a busy guy. He owned his own business and did some travelling. He often took his nephew over night to babysit when his sister had to work so Emma saw him less and less.

One Sunday after her father sold his deli, Emma had a big cook out celebration. All of her kids came, Katie with her husband Joe and little Ricky; Jessie came without her husband; and Donnie and Olivia came. Papa was there and Emma invited Jack Hynes to meet her immediate family. It was while Jessie helped Emma clean up the kitchen that she told her mother that she had filed for divorce. Her husband had taken off with some woman he worked with and told her he wasn't coming back. Jess had suspected he was cheating on her but he always denied it. They had simply fallen out of love and it was more of a relief to her than the shock one might have expected. Emma was glad to see him go, but she didn't say that to Jess. She just gave her a hug and told her that she was there if Jessie needed her.

When Emma rejoined the group out in the back yard, she noticed that Jack and Donnie were sitting side by side and deep in conversation. They looked serious.

"He is telling your friend all about his disease." Olivia said to her mother in law. "I don't know what is so special about that man but Donnie just opened up to him like they knew each other all of their lives. Now I think he's telling him that we can't have children. We've tried everything we could, Mom, but Donnie has no sperm to get me pregnant. We've been thinking about adopting."

Emma was blown away. She knew that her son wanted kids in the worst way and that they had been trying since they got married. It had to be very disheartening. But Emma had no clue that they had discussed adoption. Normally Donnie told her everything. She was taken aback by this sudden news from Olivia.

Later that evening, after all the children had gone home, Emma and Jack took a walk along the beach, holding hands.

"Your son seems like such a great guy. What a terrible disease he has. I am so sorry Emma. I assume that it hasn't been easy on him or you."

"Jack, did he mention that he was thinking of adopting?"

Emma was still puzzled why Donnie hadn't said anything to her.

"We did talk about him not being able to have children. I suggested he try a few other things before going down the adoption route. I have some connections. I gave him a person to contact to see if they might be able to help with artificial insemination. I also told him how badly I wanted children and never had them. I'm getting up there in years now, it's probably too late for me to start a family, but if the right girl comes around." He teased Emma.

"Then you better stop seeing me. I am way passed that. Been there, done that," she replied laughing.

"Well, having grandchildren is almost like having kids, but you can give them back when you get tired of them. I wouldn't mind that either. My nephew, Johnny, is my surrogate son. But my sister and I don't see eye to eye on how to raise him. She is too soft on him and he is spoiled rotten. And then when he spends time with his father, he comes home with all these gifts and he is out of control. That's normally when she dumps him on my doorstep, to be the disciplinarian. He's ten years old. He's not a baby anymore but she keeps treating him like one. It's not fair to me, so we argue about that."

She and Jack dated for several weeks, but it was evident, there was nothing serious between them, they were more like just good friends. He began to call her less often and she didn't even notice until she met him at the supermarket one day and they were both a little awkward with each other. It was even more awkward when a young blonde came around the corner and grabbed Jack by the arm, unaware that he was talking to another woman. She must have been fifteen years younger than Emma. Jack blushed, as he introduced them. The women sized each other up and down and Emma smiled.

"Good to see you my friend. Tell Johnny I said hello." Emma walked away gracefully, with her head held high. He needed a woman on his arm; arm candy. He was a good looking, gentle, busy man who needed a woman to complete him in the public eye.

Emma woke from her dream in a panic. Some machine was making a noise. What was that noise? Emma tossed the blanket off of her and went to Donnie's bedside. He was not breathing…she pressed the buzzer and ran into the hallway looking for a nurse to help her…the plug to the oxygen machine was lying on the floor. The woman who came in to dust the floors must have knocked it out. Emma was livid.

"Why didn't you hear his beeping machine?" she almost shouted when the nurse arrived. Tears streamed down her face. She thought her son was dead. She was hyperventilating. His life was so fragile. She was mad at herself for falling asleep and allowing this to happen. She was mad at the stupid woman with the mop and she was angry that the nurses weren't paying attention to their monitors.

"Mom. I'm okay. Calm down. It's okay." Donnie saw how agitated his mother was.

"It's NOT okay Donnie! This is not supposed to happen."

The nurse led her from Donnie's room and they walked out into the corridor.

"Please calm down Mrs. Clark. You are upsetting your son."

Emma just broke down and sobbed. The nurse handed her a

tissue and put her arm around her shoulders.

"I am so sorry, but everything is okay now. Your son is fine. Please try to calm down so you won't upset him." The nurse was thinking of Donnie so Emma listened.

She went back into his room and saw that he was sound asleep. She sighed with relief.

Chapter 10

September 22, 2014

Emma went home to her condo in the morning when Olivia showed up after dropping her children off at day care. She made herself a cup of tea and had a piece of toast while she turned on her laptop. She signed on to Face Book and then checked her donation website. It had only been about twenty four hours so she didn't expect much of anything but when she saw that five donations had come in, she smiled. And then she gasped. She was able to see who donated and how much they gave.

Bill and his son had donated five hundred dollars. Emma was so grateful and thought it was such a wonderful thing. Someone donated fifty dollars, another sent twenty five and then she looked to see a donation in the amount of one thousand dollars. It was from Jack Hynes, the property developer from Cape Cod. Emma put her right hand over her heart and made a mental note to call and thank him. He remembered Donnie. And then there was a hundred dollar donation from her friend Diane that she hadn't spoken to in years. Funny how your real friends show up when they are needed, no matter how long it was between conversations. She and Diane had been friends before she married Rick, long before Donnie was even born. When Emma moved to the Cape and Diane moved to Texas, they lost touch other than an occasional birthday or Christmas card.

Emma decided she'd tell Olivia about the website when she relieved her later that afternoon, but first she needed to get some sleep and primp a little before meeting Bill at three. She closed down her laptop, finished her tea and crawled into bed.

Her dreams took her back in time once again to 2008 when her father sold the deli to his chef and he moved into the cottage with Emma. She tried to get him interested in walks along the beach but he wasn't too sturdy on his feet in the sand these days. The cottage was in the next town over from the deli so he would go over to hang around once in a while, give the chef advice and help out when he could. But many days he would come back home to the cottage and he'd be agitated that things were being changed.

"If it's not broken, don't fix it," he would say to Emma while lightly pounding his fist on the table. "Why does he have to change the color of the building? Everyone knows Mack's Deli is gray and navy blue. It has always been gray with navy blue shutters and doors. What is he thinking painting it brown and gold? Those are dumb colors. This is cape cod."

Emma would try to placate him by taking him to see a movie or going someplace to eat other than the deli. She figured out one day, that selling the deli may have been a mistake. Mack had been there so long, it became his way of life. Without something to do on a daily basis, her father began to fail. He spent more time alone in his room. He fell asleep watching television in the middle of the day. Maybe the stroke and maybe his age were catching up to him, but Emma was thinking, it could be boredom or depression.

One April morning in 2009, when Emma went in to wake him up for breakfast Mack was gone. He gave up the fight to continue. His body was still there in the bed but his soul had gone on to heaven to be with his wife. That was five and half years ago. Some days it seemed like yesterday. She still missed him and thought about him every day of her life.

Less than a year later, Donnie's wife had the twins. Emma thought "if only dad was here to see them".

Donnie was still working then and he seemed to be doing fairly well with his health. Of course Olivia had to give up her job working at the grocery store in order to take care of the twins and Emma spent a great deal of time travelling from her cottage on Cape Cod to where Donnie lived in Abington, about an hour away. Many nights she slept on the sofa and got up with Olivia to help feed the babies. Donnie worked in Quincy, building and repairing computers. It was a tedious job but he was good at it and it didn't tax his body physically, just mentally. It did involve some travelling. Some days he spent more time on the road than in the office, going from site to site.

He worked for a man named Jason Doherty who took Donnie under his wing. He was branching out into diversified endeavors and he taught Donnie new computer skills to help him in his business. But having twins in the house didn't allow for a whole lot of sleep and there were times when Donnie was mentally challenged at work, so

Nana tried to be there to help a few nights a week. Donnie needed his sleep.

That winter before the babies were even a year old, Donnie got terribly sick and was hospitalized with pneumonia for the first time in many years. His doctor, Aubrey Maloney, who had been taking care of him since he was an infant, tended to him and told his wife that he had a very difficult strain. Donnie was in the hospital for almost a month.

When he was released, he was weak and unable to work full time at first. The travelling was too much for him. His boss understood but he had a business to run. Donnie either needed to get back to work full time or Jason would be forced to hire someone new. He did not want to do that and he knew Donnie needed the job so he tried to work with him.. So Donnie worked and pushed himself hard. But then he got run down and before long, he was back in the hospital.

On top of the strain of his job, Dr. Maloney told Donnie that the weather in New England was not conducive to his disease. As he aged, each winter was harder on him and cold & flu season threatened him, especially having two small children in the house. The doctor suggested that he might look into moving to a warmer climate. And then the he gave Donnie more bad news; he was retiring in the spring. He was going to do some travelling, giving lectures around the world but he would no longer be seeing patients. Donnie was crushed. He had grown to love this man and believe in him.

Dr. Maloney told Donnie that he might do well to move to Maryland near the John Hopkins University Hospital. They had a new wing that was reserved for adult Cystic Fibrosis patients. Not many hospitals knew how to treat adults with CF. The new drugs and treatments now were allowing patients with CF to live into their adult years, patients like Donnie. The doctor told Donnie that he knew of a good doctor at that hospital and he could send all of Donnie's records to him and recommend him personally. That gave Donnie and his wife something to think about. Neither of them had ever lived anywhere else besides Massachusetts but they needed to consider what was best for Donnie's health. The children were still babies, not yet in school, so the time was right to make a move. But it would mean leaving his mother and sisters. That would be very difficult. Olivia had been raised by her grandmother who had since passed away. She had no family ties to keep her in Massachusetts. Both of her parents and younger brother had been killed in an automobile accident when Liv was just ten.

The thought of her son moving to Maryland all but broke Emma's heart. She would have to move too, she thought at first. But she had her daughters and a grandchild still nearby and she had her own house by the beach and she had many clients who relied on her to do their bookkeeping. It was her income. How would she be able to start over again? She was fifty four years old; too old to start over again and too young to retire. She had a healthy savings account, thanks to inheriting her father's estate but it wasn't nearly enough to sustain her in retirement. She didn't know what she was going to do. But Donnie had to decide the future for his own family now. He would have to find a job and housing before going anywhere. He had a family to support.

Chapter 11

September 22, 2014

The alarm sounded at one forty five. Emma had been sound asleep dreaming of days gone by like she had been doing often of late. She shook off the cobwebs and hopped into a hot shower. She took her time choosing something nice to wear, but she hadn't packed a full wardrobe when she flew out to California several weeks earlier. Her choices were limited.

She dressed in Navy slacks and a pale blue and navy three quarter sleeved pull over silky top. She slipped her feet into the comfy navy wedge-heeled, open toed shoes and put on some makeup to accent her light blue eyes. Instead of pulling her auburn hair back off her neck like she usually did, she used a curling iron and let it fall where it may, just above her shoulders. She put on some diamond stud earrings and her tennis bracelet and she left her condo at two thirty five.

It was a lovely afternoon in the mid seventies. The sun was shining and the traffic on the highway wasn't too bad, so Emma made it to the restaurant with five minutes to spare. Being the middle of the afternoon, the restaurant was very quiet. They were between lunch and dinner hours so when she walked in, she was able to spot Bill right away. He waved from a booth and stood up to greet her.

Emma tried to control her breathing walking across the dining room. Her stomach was full of butterflies. How was it possible that he got more handsome with age? His hair was salt and pepper and maybe more salt than pepper. His gorgeous smile with his white straight teeth and the glimmer in his eyes was welcoming. Emma walked right into his big hug and almost melted when he kissed her on the forehead. So many years had escaped them. He could still make her heart skip a beat.

"Emma." He said softly with so much adoration. "Oh Emma, you look lovely. I'm so glad you agreed to see me." He assisted her into the booth and sat across from her.

The waitress appeared almost instantly, handing them menus and taking their drink order. They just looked into each other's eyes and smiled for the longest time.

"You look great, Billy. I was so surprised to hear your voice on the phone after all this time." Emma didn't know what to say, where to begin; how could they catch up after all this time?

They each sipped their ice teas and ordered something that neither of them intended on eating. They made small talk. He spoke of his kids and told her that his mother had passed on from a heart attack several years earlier. His daughter was married with a little girl named Molly. Her husband, Scott, was Bill's foremen for his reconstruction business. He was a good pair of hands. Loved working with wood especially. Bill was still living in his old house. He recently had it all remodeled when he finally retired from the fire department after thirty years..

He had started up a remodeling company while working full time with the fire department and he brought his son, Charlie, into business with him but then his son moved out to California with his college roommate and they went into the business out here. He paused and cleared his throat before he continued.

"Charlie is gay, Emma. It took me a long time to accept his

relationship with his partner, but he is happy and they are doing very well financially, so what can I say?" He was a little embarrassed to admit this about his son, as if he failed at being a father, but people don't choose their sexual preferences. It was no one's "fault". And Emma had known Bill's children. She saw Charlie's tendencies but it had never been discussed.

"So you still have your business going?" Emma was interested in him, not his son so much.

"Yes, I do have it but I have guys working for me and a woman who runs the office so I am free to take off whenever I feel the need. I keep in touch. Good ole technology," he joked. Bill never had been one for computers.

Emma told Bill all about Donnie and his struggles and she raved about his lovely wife and his gorgeous twins. She filled him in about Jessie and Katie and admitted that due to Donnie's illness, her girls have taken a back seat but they understood. They were both busy with their own lives. She glanced at the watch on her wrist and felt sad that time was passing so quickly.

"I need to get going. I hate for Donnie to be alone. I know it's probably silly but he's at the crossroads of his life, Bill. He could die or my prayers could be answered and a donor will be found. I just can't let him be alone…I want someone to be there with him when the call comes telling him that they found a donor." Emma smiled, thinking on a positive note. The negative side hung in the balance. She didn't want him to die alone either.

"I understand, Emma. Do you have any idea how long you will be out here? You will be coming home soon, won't you?" Bill wanted to make plans to see her when she returned to Massachusetts.

"I'll be here for as long as it takes to get him well, Billy. I may have to go home in a few weeks to check on things back home. I own a house in Yarmouth," she explained. "But if he is still in the hospital, I can't leave his wife alone with the twins."

"Can I see you again before I leave on Sunday?" He reached across the table for her hand. He brought her fingers to his mouth and kissed her hand. "I still love you, Emma. I never stopped loving you." There was a tear in his eyes and a gentle smile on his lips.

Emma hung her head, trying hard not to cry herself. "Yes, Bill, I'd love to see you again. Maybe Wednesday would be good. The twins go to day care. We can meet here again at three on Wednesday. I watch the kids on Tuesdays while Olivia goes to be with Donnie." Bill agreed to Wednesday at three.

"I'll be waiting, Emma. I'll keep your son in my prayers."

"Oh Billy, I saw your donation on his website. Thank you so very much," Emma said.

"I've contacted the old firehouse gang and told them to pass the hat and cough it up for the son of a fellow fireman…I'll take care of that donation when I get back there next week…we'll help Donnie, Emma. He deserves our help."

They hugged good bye and he walked her out to her car. Emma told him that she turns the ringer of her cell phone off in the hospital but she does read and send text messages. He laughed.

"Charlie is trying to get me up on all that stuff but I'm not too good at it. But if you send me a text, I'll try to respond." He smiled shyly at his techno ignorance.

Bill stood there and watched Emma pull away and he waved. His heart was full of love. He lost her once, this time he wasn't going to let her get away.

Emma watched him in her rearview mirror. How could she have walked away from him all those years ago? What a fool she had been. Kids grow up and move on. And here they were now, both alone and still in love with each other. She vowed once her son got his new lungs and was getting back on his feet, she'd go home and catch up with Bill if he'd still have her.

She went to visit Donnie and had just missed connecting with Olivia. She brought her son a nice sandwich from the restaurant and had her lunch packed up so she could eat with him. They could eat it later when they got hungry.

"Oh Donnie, I checked that donation website I set up for you. Bill and his son Charlie donated five hundred dollars and there were several other donations. Its beginning to catch on. And by any chance, do you remember a friend of mine, Jack Hynes?"

Donnie smiled. "Of course I do, Ma. He's a great guy. We kept in contact by email for a long time after you stopped seeing him. Why do you ask?"

Emma was a little taken aback to hear that her son had kept in contact with a man she once dated. Whatever on earth inspired that, she had no idea. So she told him about his donation.

"Oh that is just like him. He was very helpful to Olivia and I when we tried to have a baby, did you know that? Anyway, he kept in contact with me and I sent him pictures of the babies. I kind of lost track when I moved out here and got so sick. He had written a few times but I was too weak to correspond, just sent one word answers."

Just then the volunteer came in with Donnie's dinner tray so the conversation was halted. Donnie took one look at it and laughed. "Where is that sandwich you brought me, Mom?"

Chapter 12

Tuesday was her hectic day after spending the night at the hospital then watching her grandchildren during the day. She was able to get a few hours of sleep in the afternoon, in Olivia's big bed with the television on to entertain the children. They had fallen asleep too and when they woke up, they stayed in the bed like Nana told them. They were good little kids. And as a reward for behaving, Emma took them out to Dairy Queen for chocolate dipped ice cream cones. She planned ahead and brought a package of wet naps and they ate at a picnic bench outside by the fence. Emma took pictures with her iPhone of them covered in chocolate and vanilla ice cream to show Donnie when she went back to see him that evening. Then she went one step further and made a video of the children laughing and enjoying their treat with Nana. Donnie would love that.

When they got back to their townhouse, Emma had the children change their clothes and she did a load of laundry for Olivia. She didn't want Mommy to see the mess they made with the chocolate.

The babysitter showed up at four so Emma could go home to shower and change her own clothes. Olivia had a few errands to run when she left the hospital and she was going to pick up some takeout food for herself and the children on her way home. She told the babysitter she shouldn't be much later than six. The ice cream was going to hold them over until Liv got home with dinner.

After her shower, Emma made herself and Donnie a couple of ham and swiss cheese sandwiches to take into the hospital to eat dinner later in the evening. She grabbed a cup of dark steaming coffee in her travel mug and was out the door before five.

On her way she called Olivia to see how the day went. She could tell by Liv's sniffles that it was not a good day for Donnie. They did more testing that wore him out. He was struggling just to get up to use the bathroom, he almost had an accident because he waited too long to attempt to go. From lying in bed so long, his leg muscles have become very weak and he now needed help just to take a few steps.

"Oh Mom. I am so worried about him. I try so hard not to show my concerns but he sees it all over my face and that scares him even more. I don't know what to do anymore. Some days, I dread coming in here." Olivia wept over the phone.

Her crying pulled at Emma's heart strings. They both felt so helpless. All they could do was pray and wait, pray and wait. Meanwhile life went on all around them and the daily bills kept pouring in.

Emma knew, only too well, what it was like to be alone and facing financial stress with small children to take care of. She had been so fortunate to have her father's help. She was doing all she could but it was never enough, could never be enough with this dreadful disease.

She parked the car and decided to check online via her cell phone, to see how the donation website was doing. GoFundMe.com was a popular site but you had to get it out there to the public. Emma had posted it on Face Book but she didn't know where else to turn, where else she could post it, looking for financial assistance for her son and his family. When she had told Olivia about it, she saw mixed emotions in her daughter in law. It wasn't easy asking strangers for money. But they had little choice.

Emma was surprised to see that there were a few more donations that had come in since she checked it this morning. It wasn't a huge help, but no amount could be too small. Every donation counted. Donnie's family was depending on it to help pay their bills while they were unable to work as well as the growing medical bills. He did have Medicaid and a supplemental insurance but their co-pays were still huge with all the testing and treatments and costly medicines he needed to keep him alive. When someone is that ill, the last thing in the world he needed was the stress of lack of funds for his family. And when you lie in a hospital bed unable to get up and move, all you have is your mind and the time to think about things like that. Donnie was getting very depressed.

Just as Emma was about to shut down her phone, it rang in her hand. It was Bill.

"Emma, hi. I'm so glad I caught you before you went to the hospital."

Emma explained that she was in the parking lot about to go inside.

"Okay listen, I'll be brief but I've got some exciting news. I don't want to go into details now, I'll explain everything when I see you for lunch tomorrow but I just want you to know that things are going to be okay. Just give Donnie my best and tell him I'm here to help. I'm working on something with Charlie to help him and his family. It's going to be all right, Emma. Trust me. I'm here for you. I'll let you go. I love you."

Before Emma could find her voice, Bill disconnected. She had no idea what he was talking about. He spoke in riddles but somehow, it gave her a lift. She put a smile on her face and grabbed her little brown lunch bag and went to see Donnie.

Chapter 13

Emma was so excited to meet Bill the next day that she arrived twenty minutes early and he walked in right behind her. He smiled his huge big tooth grin as he approached her sitting in a booth, their booth. He bent over and kissed her quickly and slipped into the seat opposite her and reached for her hands.

"I have some wonderful news for you, Emma. I feel so happy I am giddy to be able to help." His deep blue eyes looked right into her eyes. Emma was thinking he was probably the most handsome man she had ever known. Why hadn't she seen that before?

The waitress appeared at their table. "Our special today is chicken parmesan with assorted oven roasted vegetables and potatoes mixed together. It's delicious."

Emma said she'd have the chicken Caesar salad and a chicken parmesan dinner to go when they were ready to leave, for Donnie. Bill had the Caesar salad with steak tips, medium rare, and two iced teas.

"So tell me, you are keeping me in suspense. What is this great news, Billy?"

"Emma." Bill paused. "I just don't even know where to start."
He smiled.

The waitress returned to serve them their iced teas. Bill waited
until she left.

"Let me start at the beginning and forgive me for dragging this
along, but I don't want to leave anything out." Bill paused again,
gathering his thoughts.

"After I left you the other day, I went back to my son's
apartment and both he and his partner," Bill got flustered. "I don't
know what to call him, his name is Lenny. So both Charlie and Lenny
were there, sitting around having a glass of wine. They invited me to
sit down and join them and asked me how our lunch date went. I
laughed and said it wasn't really a date and they teased me. Okay, so it
WAS a date, I gave in. But I digress." Bill took a sip of his iced tea.
Emma was sitting on pins and needles waiting for this big news he was
about to tell her.

"I told them about Donnie. I told them how worried you were
and the stress of finances weighing on all of you. I had told Charlie

about him and the donation website a day earlier but after talking to you, I went into a little more detail. And they both fell silent and then started asking me more questions. They were truly interested and inquisitive. Well one thing led to another and it was like a light went on with Lenny."

"Did I tell you, Emma that Lenny is in show business? He writes plays and he's directed a few skits. Anyway, he has a lot of connections out here, that's why he and Charlie moved here to L.A.. And you know Charlie worked with me in construction, right? Well Charlie builds sets for these plays that Lenny is involved with among other things. They do very well. They're successful out here, Emma and they know EVERYBODY!"

At that point, the waitress carried their salads to the table and freshened their teas.

"I'll put that order for the take out dinner in when you want. I don't want it to get cold." The waitress was very considerate.

"Oh you can put it in now. We'll just microwave it when he's ready to eat. Thank you very much." Emma replied, anxiously trying to get rid of her so she could find out more from Bill.

"Emma, I am learning from Charlie and Lenny, especially in their field, these people out here in LA are all looking for something. They are looking for a good play to write or a great new TV show or a cause; a charity that they can sink their teeth into.

Lenny wants to focus on Donnie and Cystic Fibrosis. He wants to bring awareness to this horrible disease and in so doing, he will raise funds for Donnie and his family. He knows a television producer who would love to get his hands on something like this, a human interest story; and he knows a guy who writes for the paper and another person who is a DJ on a radio network. The two of them know so many people and they want to get involved, Emma. They too want to help your son, and further the cause. But to do that, they need to get up close and personal with you, Donnie and his family. I'm not sure Donnie is strong enough to deal with this, but maybe his wife would be willing to fill in the gaps. And WHEN Donnie gets the call for new lungs, they want to be there with him, hundreds of people there with him, to back him and give him the financial and moral support he and his family will need. They are the answers for your secondary prayers, Emma. I know you need a donor, first and foremost, but until that day comes, they can spread the word. They can help fund Donnie's family while you all wait so patiently."

Bill reached for Emma's hands and squeezed them, looking into her face with tears in his blue eyes. He was so full of love and hope it was contagious.

"What do you think, Emma? Will Donnie accept help from the outside?"

Emma was so choked up she could barely breathe, never mind speak. Tears swam in her eyes and slid down her face. She squeezed Bill's hands while trying to find the words to reply.

"Oh Billy boy. I don't know what to say other than thank you. Donnie was embarrassed and a little ticked at me for setting up that donation website. At first. But he came to grips with it because he knows he has no way to support his family right now. He is ashamed and feels like a failure for not being able to take care of his family and he is so grateful for my help. But Billy, he has no choice in this matter.

He NEEDS to accept outside help. He'd be a fool to even think otherwise. Bill, will you come with me to the hospital and explain it to him like you did to me? We'll say you are his uncle from Massachusetts. Please come with me and help me convince him it's the beginning of the help he so desperately needs."

"Of course I'll come. Let me text Charlie. Yes, text I said," and Bill laughed. "I'll tell him I'm going to talk to Donnie but we want him to start putting things into motion. Spread the word. At least get donations pouring into that website for starters. Okay?"

Emma nodded as she reached for her napkin to wipe her eyes.

Chapter 14

Donnie was sitting up in his chair beside the bed when his
mother and Bill came into his room. He was expecting his mother but
no one else ever came to visit. He had not seen Bill since he was a
child and at first, he didn't recognize him until he saw the man smile.

"Uncle Billy," Donnie called out, extending his hand for a
shake. He had always called him that even though they weren't blood
related. "What a surprise." Donnie was smiling from ear to ear. It
warmed Emma's heart.

Donnie started to stand but Emma told him not to. He was
dressed in hospital pajamas with a blanket over his legs. Donnie was
always cold. He was thin and frail.

One of the nurses brought in a folding chair for Donnie's
visitor and Emma sat in her reclining chair that was by the window.
They rearranged the furniture a little so all three of them were in a
semi circle. They exchanged pleasantries and warm greetings.

"Did Mom tell you that I named my son after you? His name is
Billy Richard Clark." Donnie was proud to brag to this man about his

son. "My daughter's name is Beth," he added just to fill in the missing link.

Donnie began to cough. He could talk very little without coughing. Emma reached for his glass and Donnie took a sip of water from the tray beside his bed.

"Donnie. Bill has some wonderful news for you. He just told me over lunch and I brought him here to explain it all to you. Wait til you hear what he can do for you. For us."

Bill explained it all over again and he tried to compose himself, and not get as excited as he was when he told Emma. He didn't want to upset or excite Donnie. He explained it calmly, in a matter of fact kind of way. Donnie never interrupted; he just listened. Then he took another sip of his water and a few deep breaths through the tubes in his nose, getting as much oxygen in as he could muster. His head was hung, his chin almost on his chest. Emma and Bill sat silently, allowing Donnie to absorb it all.

When Donnie looked up, tears overflowed and he could barely speak, but he said "Thanks Uncle Billy. I love you. God bless you"

Emma rose from her seat and grabbed the box of tissues from the shelf. She passed a few to her son and took one for herself. Bill reached out his hand because he too was crying. "I love you too, Donnie. I always had a special place in my heart for you."

Bill's only son was gay. He would have raised Donnie like his own and it might have been a special bond that Bill lacked with Charlie.

Emma realized right then and there that she had made a huge mistake by not following her heart and staying with Bill. He could've been the father that Donnie never had. Papa was a great help but Donnie never had a man in his life like a dad. It should have been Bill.

We all make choices and decisions we think are for the best but there are times that we can't see the forest through the trees. Emma had made a grave mistake when she walked away from Bill and she would regret it for as long as she lived. But fortunately they had found each other again and this time, she would not turn her back on him.

Bill left after a short visit and he said he was going to go home and see what he could do to help Charlie and Lenny set the wheels in motion. Bill had to leave to fly home in a few days so there wasn't much time for him to lend a helping hand.

Donnie was overwhelmed with all that Bill had told him. He wanted to talk to his wife and discuss it. Emma knew he needed time to be alone to make that emotional call so she went to the cafeteria to get a cup of coffee and give her son some privacy. She hadn't even told him what she brought him for his dinner as yet, but knew, there would be plenty of time to eat later. Donnie was flying high at the moment. He had hope. A great deal of stress and worry would soon be lifted.

When Emma returned, Donnie was back in his bed with his full oxygen mask on. His eyes were heavy from the tears he had shed talking to Olivia.

"I texted both Jessie and Katie while I was in the cafeteria to tell them the good news." Emma told her son. "Jess called me to get more information. She was so happy for you, but I noticed something in her voice that wasn't just right. I asked her if she was okay and she said she was fine. Have you talked to her lately?"

"Only texting with her. She didn't say much. Now that you mention it, she was very short in her texts. I wonder if Katie knows what's going on?" Donnie had his own problems but he still worried about his sisters back in Massachusetts.

"Donnie, I brought you a nice dinner but you look like you need to rest a while first. Do you want me to turn down the lights and pull the shade?"

"Yes, Mom, please. I do need to rest a bit. Mom, thanks for everything." He gave a little smile as his heavy eyelids closed. His chest heaved in and out with each breath. Then he coughed and fell asleep.

Emma sat back in her chair and pulled out her cell phone to check for emails and as curiosity grabbed her, she decided to check the donation website again. Money had already begun to pour in. Bless Billy and his son and Lenny. That worry was squelched for the time being, so now she needed to concentrate on her prayers for a donor.

Her phone pinged with an incoming text from Katie. She told Emma to send her love to her brother. Short and sweet. Emma wrote back. "Is everything okay with Jess?"

"Don't worry Ma, it's just boy problems. She and the dick head she was seeing broke up. Good riddens. He was a loser. She sure does know how to pick them." Emma smiled at her response, as long as it was nothing serious, all is well.

Emma was reading a paperback book when Donnie opened his eyes.

"Ma, I'm starving. Do you think you can heat up whatever you brought for my supper? I didn't even look at the slop they sent up on my tray, did you?"

Emma laughed. She checked and was glad she brought him something good. It was almost seven o'clock. Emma took the Styrofoam box down to the nurses' station to use their microwave to heat Donnie's chicken parmesan. When she returned, he was sitting up in his chair with his nose cannula instead of his mask, ready to eat. He was starving. The smell filled the room and it made Emma hungry again. Something about excitement makes a person want to eat. She picked at the crackers from Donnie's food tray still at his bedside table. She refilled Donnie's jug with ice water and got herself a cup of coffee from the vending machine down the hall. It tasted like mud, but it was hot.

As hungry as Donnie was, he couldn't finish the large portion of chicken, but he ate all the roasted vegetables and potatoes. Something different and tasty. Definitely Italian seasoning involved. Donnie loved them. Emma finished his chicken with the rest of the Caesar salad she had wrapped to go.

"Just like old times, huh Ma? Whatever the kids didn't finish, you'd eat it for them. How come you never sat down with your own plate?"

"I don't know Donnie. I guess I was always busy doing something. I probably should have sat down with you kids like a family more often but I was too preoccupied most of the time with one thing or another."

"You were worried about your girlish figure, I know." Donnie

134

teased her and made her smile in agreement.

Emma cleaned up and helped Donnie into the bathroom so he could wash up before getting back into bed. Just as he came out of the bathroom, gasping for a breath, his cell phone began to ring. He motioned for his mother to get it for him as he stood, holding on to the chair.

"Hello," he barely was able to say loud enough to be heard. And then he coughed.

Emma held out his water to him and he sipped it through a straw.

"I'm in the hospital, doc. How do you think I'm doing?" He joked with his doctor on the phone. Always kept that good sense of humor. Almost always.

"Doc, don't tease me. Are you freaking kiddin' me?"

Emma saw her son pale then flush and his hands began to tremble. Oh no, what now? But then she saw a smile emerge across her son's handsome face. And more tears filled his eyes.

"I'll be here when you get here. Thanks Doc." He disconnected and handed his phone back to his mother as he shuffled back to bed.

"Donnie. What did the doctor say?" Emma was clueless and yet hopeful.

"I guess that today is my lucky day Mom. They found me a Donor!!" and he burst into tears and cried like a baby. They were happy tears. Prayers are answered tears. His shoulders shook as he hugged his mother while she cried with him.

"I need to call Liv. Oh Mom. Wait til Livvy hears this. Will you call Bill for me?"

Donnie was breathing in and out, his whole body was trembling; his chest was heaving.

"The doctor is on his way to talk to us. I want Liv here. Oh Mom. Can you believe it? Bill finds funding for me and doc finds me a donor, all in the same day."

Donnie took a huge breath, raised his head up and right out loud he said his thanks. "Dear Lord. I knew you didn't forget about me. Thank You, Jesus."

Chapter 15

By the time Dr. Tessler walked into Donnie's room, Olivia had arrived after her babysitter agreed to spend the night with the children. Mother, son and his wife were all restless and anxious and nervous and excited. Emma paced back and forth while waiting for the doctor to arrive. The second he entered the room, there was silence and the little family huddled together at Donnie's bedside.

The doctor walked up to his patient and shook his hand, smiling broadly.

"I just met with your transplant team, Donnie, and they are trying to get everything set up. This will take several hours as the donor has many organs to pass along to other needy patients. Please try to relax."

"Doctor, with these new lungs, does that mean my husband will be cured?" Olivia asked sheepishly, hoping for a positive answer.

"My dear, *we still have no cure for Cystic Fibrosis. CF is incurable.*" He said the words slowly and clearly. Emma remembered that cold winter's night in his hospital room in Boston when she first heard those dreadful words being uttered and Emma shuttered.

"We are working on it and we have come a very long way since the day when Donovan was diagnosed however, we still have a long way to go to find a cure. Perhaps one day we shall see that cure but it is not possible today, I'm afraid. However, he will have a new beginning and a second chance at life."

His doctor went on to explain what they might expect to happen next and over the next few days. When he left the room, his instructions were for Donnie to get some rest because he was going to need all of his strength to fight through this long, difficult surgery. They all held hands and said a prayer.

A few minutes later one of Donnie's nurses came into the room. She was beaming. "I just got the good news Donnie. No one deserves it more than you. I'm so happy for you." She reached over and kissed his cheek.

Donnie never complained and he always had a smile for everyone who was there to help him. The nurses loved him.

"Ladies, the doctor told me to give Donnie a shot to help him rest. This surgery won't take place for another ten to twelve hours. There is so much to prepare to do first. So you ladies can stay if you wish, but I'd suggest you go home and get some rest yourselves. This shot I'm about to give Donnie will put him down for a good six hours anyway. You've been with him every minute of every day. Take this time to go home. Rest. Pray and trust that I will be right here with him the whole time." Nurse Debbie smiled and hugged both Emma and Olivia.

Mother and Wife both kissed Donnie, promising to return a few hours later and they left the room so Debbie could roll the patient over to give him a shot in the butt. He was asleep within minutes.

The women each drove back to Olivia's house in separate cars. At that time of night, the highway traffic was light so it only took about half an hour. Olivia let the babysitter go home and Emma said she would stay with the children in the morning to get them off to preschool. Then she would join Olivia back at the hospital. The babysitter said she'd be back to watch the children when they got home at three. Olivia went upstairs and picked Beth up from her bed, carried the sleeping child into her bed with her and let Emma crawl

into her granddaughter's bed. When Emma was alone, she called Bill.

She spoke softly and filled him in as to what was happening.

Anxiety was high but the ladies were both emotionally drained

and knew there would be many hours to go without sleep the next day.

Surgery would take anywhere from eight to twelve hours depending

on complications.

Donnie had always followed his doctors orders, always took

his medicines on time and used his nebulizers; before he got too sickly

he worked out with his P90X to keep his upper respiratory in good

working order. His heart was in good shape. He was physically strong

if it weren't for his dreadful disease. He was heading into this surgery

in the best condition he could possibly be in. And yet, there was

always that feeling of 'what if...'.

Donnie would be cut from armpit to armpit. They needed to

remove the old lungs one at a time and replace them with the new

lungs. There had been so many obstacles to find just the right ones.

Not only does the donor have to be the right blood match but he has to be the correct size. Donnie was tall for a patient with CF. He was five

ten. His donor would have to be between five eight and six foot one in

order for the lungs to fit properly in Donnie's chest cavity. Both lungs

would have to be thoroughly examined before the surgery could

progress to make sure they were healthy. Donnie could be prepped and

ready to go and if the lungs had a defect, the surgery would be

cancelled. There was so much stress involved. Emma was surprised

that she was able to sleep at all but five hours later she woke up with a

jolt when she heard Beth's voice saying "Nana, you are sleeping in my

big girl's bed."

Beth woke up in her mother's bed and didn't know where she

was at first. She went to the bathroom then wandered back to her own

bed where Nana pulled her in beside her and snuggled her up close.

"Go back to sleep Princess. It's not morning just yet."

That was the end of sleep for Emma. She tip toed out of Beth's

room and snuck down the stairs and called the hospital. Donnie was

still sleeping, she was told. So she put on a pot of coffee and jumped

when she felt, rather than heard, Olivia come up behind her. They pulled up a stool at the breakfast counter and each had a cup of coffee, lost deep in their own thoughts. It was almost five in the morning when Olivia went back upstairs to shower and get dressed for the long day ahead.

Emma waited at the curb with her grandchildren until the mini bus picked them up for school at seven forty five. She was all dressed and ready to go as soon as the children were safely on the bus. She got to the hospital on automatic pilot, talking on the phone via blue-tooth, to Bill, then to Katie. Jess didn't answer her phone so Emma sent her a text before she went inside.

Donnie and Olivia were sitting there, holding hands saying prayers when Emma entered the room.

"Good Morning, Mom." Donnie greeted her. Emma kissed his cheek.

"G'mornin' Donovan Richard." Emma smiled, pulling over a chair on the opposite side of the bed from Liv.

"How are you feeling after your nice sleep? Are you as

nervous as Liv and me?" She reached over to push his hair back off his forehead.

"No, Mom. Surprisingly not too bad. I've waited so damn long for this, I just want to move on and get it behind me so I can go on living again." He was sincere.

By nine that morning, things began to happen. The transplant team came by to talk to him and doctors and nurses were checking his vitals and starting to get him ready to be moved for prep.

Emma's cell phone vibrated. It was Jessie texting her mother, asking her to call her. Emma called and Jessie was crying.

"Is it too late, Momma? Have they taken Donnie to surgery yet? I didn't get to wish him luck and tell him that I love him." She was in a panic.

Emma handed the phone to Donnie and he busted her chops like he always did.

"So you were too busy sleeping rather than talk to me, huh?" They talked for a few minutes then a nurse came in to say it's time to go...so he ended his call to his big sister saying "I'll talk to you in a few days, gotta go now, love ya."

He kissed Olivia and squeezed her hand. He kissed his mother and a tear slid down the side of his face. "Love you, Mom. Be brave. I'll see you soon."

The nurse rolled him away and another nurse told the women to go to the family waiting room or to the cafeteria and be prepared for a long wait. She added that they could go home and they'd call, but neither of the women wanted to take that chance and leave. They would keep each other company and help pass the time away together.

"Let's go grab a cup of coffee in the cafeteria and maybe a danish." Emma suggested. Olivia nodded in agreement.

They stopped at the nurses' station to inform them where they would be if they were needed. The nurse took their cell phone numbers and told them they would be notified once they knew if the surgery was a go or not, depending on the donor's lungs. She told the women that at the same time, this donor was also giving hope for a new life to a patient who needed a heart and another who needed his kidneys, so that is what was taking so long, to get all the surgical teams ready for this major procedure. The patient who needed the kidneys was being medi-flighted in from another hospital. It was amazing.

"Don't you wish everyone would be a donor to help save lives?" she said.

The two women took their time drinking their coffee and picking at food that neither of them could eat. And they talked softly. They told stories to one another about the man that they both loved.

"I'll never forget," Emma began. "The first time I ever saw Donnie bleeding from his mouth. I was not prepared for that. I thought he was going to die." She took a second to compose herself. She closed her eyes for a minute and she could see it all over again.

"I was working in the kitchen of my dad's deli. Donnie had been in school all day. He didn't want to go to school that morning saying he didn't feel well, but he went. He came in the side door to the kitchen, knowing I always did some prep work at that time, and he had his hands covering his face. I thought I saw blood on his fingers. He didn't speak a word, just ran right upstairs to the apartment.

I knew something was wrong because normally when he got home from school he was hungry and wanted me to fix him a snack. So I told the other cook I was working with, that I'd be back in a few minutes. I went up the back stairs and found him in the bathroom, head leaning over the sink and blood was pouring out of his nose and mouth. I gasped and just about fainted. I had no idea what to do. He had nose bleeds before but I never saw it come from his throat. I was in a panic, but I didn't want to frighten him more than he already was. He was only about twelve."

Emma paused and took a sip of her coffee that was getting cold.

"What did you do, Mom?" Emma loved how her daughter in law called her Mom. It made her feel special, knowing Olivia's mother had been dead for many years.

"I ran to the kitchen and got some ice cubes and put them into a clean dish towel then wet the towel and brought it back to him. I put it against the back of his neck at first then moved it to his throat as the bleeding began to stop. His hands were covered in the blood, as was

146

the front of his shirt and his face, so I wet a face cloth and started to wash his face. He washed his own hands and went into his bedroom. I propped some pillows up so he wouldn't lie flat and swallow any blood. I told him to try to rest sitting up. I refreshed the dish towel and put it around his neck and the face cloth on his forehead and I called his doctor. He explained that this was common. "Common?" I said. "Are you kidding me?"

"He explained that Donnie must have been coughing more than normal, and the lining of his throat, the membranes were breaking down, raw from irritation and infection. He called in a prescription for him and told me to bring him in the next day."

The two women sat in silence for a while thinking about Donnie and all that he had to endure over the years. Olivia told Emma about the first time she witnessed him bleeding like that and how frightened she was at the sight.

They told war stories and eventually it gave wave to funny stories and talked about his never ending gift for humor and his unrelenting faith in God.

"His faith is what gets him through this, Mom." Olivia told Emma. "And your love and mine. He fights for us as much as for himself, maybe more." She was right.

Olivia's cell rang. It was the nurse from the eighth floor.

"We just got the word. The donor's lungs are perfect. Surgery is a GO!" She sounded exuberant. They were all cheering for Donnie too.

The women mosied along up to the family waiting room. They made small talk with some of the other people. They paced the floor. They sat and read magazines. They texted on their phones. They paced some more. Little by little, one by one, the other relatives were called to go see their patient and still Emma and Olivia waited. The wait was excruciating.

At three thirty Olivia stepped outside to call the babysitter at home to make sure the kids were okay. At four, Emma stepped outside to call Bill and tell him they were still waiting without any word. They chatted briefly. He could tell her nerves were on edge. He told her that he was on his way over to sit with her. He had been trying to get things set up with Charlie and Lenny for the follow up after the surgery. It just happened so quickly they hadn't found time to make plans.

At five o'clock a doctor came into the room, dressed in scrubs. Emma and Olivia were both dozing in their seats. Bill saw the doctor coming and gave Emma a little shake. Olivia sensed commotion and sat up immediately. He walked over to them and quietly sat down in an unoccupied chair.

"Just going to give you an update. All is going extremely well. There have been no complications. The lungs look great. His heart is sound. We still have a way to go but we are getting there. He's doing just fine." He patted Emma's hand and returned to the OR.

Both women hugged each other and cried and said prayers of thanks.

Emma texted her daughters to give them the update. She paced up and down the hallway as she talked. She was exhausted and anxious and couldn't wait for this to be over. Bill texted Charlie. Charlie told him that they were planning on visiting Donnie with a cameraman once they got the clear to do so, to get his story out there…

Emma said it could be a few more hours before they would be done with surgery and then they'd keep him sedated for at least twenty four hours until they were sure he could breathe on his own. They expected he'd be in the hospital for at least a month. There was plenty of time to get a camera crew in to interview him.

Bill asked if Lenny could meet them in the family waiting room and interview them while they waited. It would help pass the time and get the story started. Emma didn't see why not, other than they both looked like hell. She told him, no cameras. He laughed

Lenny and Charlie arrived less than forty minutes later. Lenny had a small recorder with him. He asked them both questions. Other family members who had replaced the ones that left, sat around and listened. Lenny was sharp. He decided to include some of them and asked which ones knew about Cystic Fibrosis. They heard of the disease but not one of them really knew what it entailed. So he asked Emma to briefly explain what CF was and how it had affected her son. This was going to be for awareness after all.

The next two hours flew by with Lenny's help. Emma was sitting by the window at seven fourteen, yes, 7:14 when Donnie's surgeon walked into the room. Lenny switched his recorder on to get the results of the nine and half hour surgery.

"It is over. He is doing remarkably well, better than could be expected. He is breathing with his new lungs!. Everyone in the waiting room cheered. Bill pulled Emma into a big hug and kissed her. Emma then turned to Liv and have her a big hug, then both women shook the doctor's hand and thanked him.

"Give us an hour or so and then you each can go into see him one at a time for five minutes. He needs to get his strength. This was a very big operation." Coming from a surgeon you know it had to be difficult.

Emma bowed her head and gave another prayer of thanks. And then she walked out into the hallway to call her daughters with the wonderful news. HE BREATHES!

Chapter 16

When Olivia came out of her husband's room, her face was stark white and Emma noticed that she was trembling. Liv walked up to her mother in law and put her arms around her to hug her.

"Be strong, Mom. It is so hard to see him like that." Liv kissed Emma's cheek and walked away, letting Emma enter the ICU room, which was like being in a fish tank, surrounded by people who were observing and watching the monitors.

The women had to dress in paper protective garments and wear a mask in order to keep the room as germ free as possible. Germs were the enemy now more than before.

A plastic tube was taped to his face to keep the breathing apparatus in place. There were blue square machines on both sides of her son with plastic tubes attached to him, monitoring all of his vitals and more. He was in a medically induced catonic state. They did not want him to wake up. The machines were keeping him alive so that his body could heal and adjust to the trauma that he just endured. He was in a coma.

The machines beeped and hissed and made all kinds of strange noises and her son lie in the bed, motionless. Dr. Tessler walked silently into the room and put his hand on Emma's shoulder.

"He is doing beautifully, Emma. If we could have handpicked those new lungs just for him, they wouldn't be as perfect as the ones now in his chest. Everything just fit into place without a hitch. But as you know, the next twenty four hours are critical." His voice was no louder than a whisper. "Go home now, Emma. Go home and rest. We will call you if there is any change but he will not wake up for another day or two. You need your rest to keep you strong. He will need both you and his wife once he is allowed to come back into consciousness. He will be in great pain for several days but we'll keep him heavily medicated to help. We will take one day at a time and see how he progresses but he should be here for another three to four weeks, maybe longer. Then he will need to go to rehab for a few weeks, to get his muscles to work again. He's been weak and laid up for such a long time; he will need help for quite a while." The doctor patted her shoulder and again, told her to go home.

Emma found Olivia in the waiting room. Her eyes were red from crying but she smiled and hugged Emma and they were silent, rocking back and forth. The men left to go home when Emma and Olivia went to the recovery room where Donnie was.

"Let's go home, Olivia. He's in God's hands now. We need to get some rest."

"I've never been a very religious person," Olivia told her mother in law, "but isn't it funny how you cling to a higher power when there is nothing else you can do? I guess that's why Donnie has such strong faith."

The women walked outside to their cars to go home. Emma was actually going home to her own place tonight. Bill asked her to call him when she got home if she wasn't too tired. Lenny and Charlie had gone quickly to write up a short story that would be printed in the local newspaper the following morning. "Man gets new Lungs to breathe".

Emma started her car and used the blue tooth to make a call to Bill. She was tired but it was only nine o'clock. They chatted while she drove home. He offered to meet her there if she wanted company but she said she just wanted a cup of tea and to climb into bed. The past few days had done a number on her. She was bone tired.

"I'm not as young as I used to be. These roller coaster emotions are playing havoc with my body," she confessed. He chuckled, knowing the feeling of age. "I'll call you if I hear anything otherwise I'll talk to you tomorrow, Bill. Thank you for being there for me, and for Donnie's family."

Emma unlocked her front door and turned on some lights. The place was so quiet and lonely. Maybe she should have asked Bill to come over? She went to the small kitchen and made herself a cup of tea with honey and sat down to call her girls.

Jessie's cell went straight to voice mail so Emma knew it was turned off. Very unusual since she knew Donnie was having his surgery. Next she called Katie. It rang three times.

"Hi Mom. How did it go? How's Donnie?" You could tell that she was anxious for news. Emma smiled and took a sip of her hot tea.

"He is in recovery, Katie. His doctor said he did remarkably well. They've got him in a medically induced coma so he won't wake up for twenty four hours." Emma went on to give Katie more information.

"Have you talked to Jessie today? I tried calling her but she's not answering?"

There was some hesitation. "Um, she's not feeling well, Mom. I took her to the ER today. They gave her a shot and put her on IV fluids for a few hours. She's sleeping in our den, as a matter of fact. Don't worry about her. I'll take care of her. You have other things on your plate, as usual." Katie regretted the last two words as soon as she said them.

"What do you mean, as usual, Katie? What's that all about? What's wrong with Jessie and why didn't she tell me she was sick. I spoke to her earlier, before the surgery." Emma was a little ticked off at Katie's attitude.

"Oh nothing. She just has a bad case of the flu. Not to worry Mother." Katie was mad at herself for speaking out. Now she knew she had to pay the piper.

"Katie, what's the matter? Is something wrong? What's with the "mother" bit?"

"Oh nothing, nothing. Guess I was just more worried about Donnie than I thought," she tried to blow it off.

"Katie, are you drinking? You are pregnant. You shouldn't be drinking."

"Yes, Mother, as a matter of fact I am. So let's just move on, okay?" She was flippant with her mother, unfeeling for what she had gone through the past few days.

"Katie I don't need attitude. I've been through a very long day. I just wanted to tell you that your brother is doing well. What is going on with you and Jess?"

"Not to worry, Mom, really. We take care of each other like we've always done. You have Donnie to take care of. He is your primary concern so Jess and me, well, we've learned to watch out for each other. That's all. I guess you never noticed."

"Where is your husband, Katie? Can I talk to him please?" Emma was fuming at her daughter's tone of voice. She was also hurt beyond compare. It had been such a joyous, miraculous occasion and now to get this attitude from her daughter? Emma was livid. She couldn't believe what she was hearing. Was Katie jealous of the attention Donnie was getting? How could she be so selfish?

"He's not home. I don't know where he is. Okay now? He went out with some guys after work and hasn't come home and Jessie is very sick and little Ricky is driving me crazy and I've had a few glasses of wine and I'm a bit emotional worrying about my brother. I'm six months pregnant. That's what this is all about. Can we talk in the morning, Mom? I'm sorry." Katie began to cry.

"Yes Katie. I'll call you tomorrow. Put the wine away and go to bed."

"Yes, Mother. I will." The connection was then disconnected.

Emma dumped the remainder of her tea down the drain and hopped into a hot shower and then went to bed. With her head spinning, she thought she'd never sleep but her eyes were closed before her head hit the pillow. She was drained of all energy and she slept like a log until the sun peeked through her blinds the next morning.

She washed up and put on some clothes and went into the kitchen to get something to eat. She realized that she hadn't had much to eat the previous day, in fact, she couldn't remember the last time she ate. She put the kettle of water on to boil and her cell phone rang. It was Bill.

"Good Morning, Emma. Are you awake? I've got some hot coffee and donuts and the newspaper. I'm on my way over to show you the article Lenny got printed in today's paper. It's great, Emma. Wait til you see it." Bill was such an uplifting influence in her life. She smiled and turned the kettle off. Bill was just exactly what she needed right now.

Knowing he was on his way over, Emma scrambled up some eggs with cheddar cheese to have with the donuts he was carrying. She needed protein to go with those carbs. He was delighted to see her cooking eggs. He too was starving, and hadn't realized it until he walked in and smelled food cooking.

It was a great story, done well without invading too much

privacy. The main thing was to call awareness to this horrible *incurable* disease but also to raise funds to help Donnie's family pay all their medical bills and living expenses.

That made Emma remember, she hadn't checked the donation website for a few days. When she opened up the link she almost cried. Her hands covered her mouth as she gasped. There was over fifty thousand dollars raised to help fund her son and his family. She was so incredibly moved, she thought her heart would stop.

Bill told her, along with the article in the paper, a friend of Charlie's is a DJ on a night time talk radio station here in LA and he has been broadcasting about Donnie's situation. He accepts callers. People have been calling in and offering prayers and well wishes and he has broadcasted the website every hour during the night. Many of those donations came from that talk show. Emma couldn't respond with the lump in her throat. It was just so remarkable how people could come together to help a stranger. And then she thought about her conversation with Katie the night before and it angered her that her own flesh and blood could be so self centered when perfect strangers were sending their hard earned money to help her son.

Bill reminded Emma that he was leaving that night on the Red Eye, back to Boston. He told her that he'd check on her house or her daughters if she needed him to do that.

"Thanks Bill. I have a neighbor watching my house and my daughters seem to be able to take care of themselves." The way she said it, Bill knew there was something wrong. He asked her what happened and she told him the story.

"Try not to let it upset you, Emma. It was probably just the wine talking." He knew Emma had been hurt by her daughter's harsh words.

"Normally when people are drunk, Bill, they say what they really feel. Don't forget, I worked in my father's restaurant for many years and I have seen it all."

Bill knew better than to try to comfort her; he knew that she was angry as she had every right to be.

"Well, give her a call and see how things are today. Call me if you need me, I'll get out of your way so you can get back to the hospital. Hope all goes well today. I'll come visit you later this afternoon before I head to the airport." Bill kissed her quickly and left.

Emma felt bad that she allowed her feelings for Katie to get in the way of their last time alone together before he had to leave. She didn't know when she'd be able to go back home and see him again. She knew when he came to the hospital, she wouldn't have much time to talk to him alone. But first things first. She called Olivia to see how she was doing with the kids.

Next she called the nurses' station on the eighth floor. She knew the number by heart from all the time Donnie spent there.

"Oh Mrs. Clark, Donnie will not be coming back to our floor. He is no longer considered a CF patient. He is now a 'post transplant' patient." There was a smile in her voice. "Let me transfer you to ICU and see if they can help you. He'll be in ICU for a while. Please hold on."

Emma hadn't even considered the fact that Donnie would no longer be treated by the nurses he had come to know so well. It was strange to hear Debbie say he was no longer considered a Cystic

Fibrosis patient, after all, he did still have the disease. He would always have the disease. It is ***incurable.*** Having new lungs was like he was getting a second chance on life but he would still carry the disease. He still would take medicine because he had no digestive enzymes. He would still have to be careful of mucus that could clog his new lungs and vital organs. Having new lungs didn't wipe away the disease, it would just make his life easier to breathe and it could and hopefully would extend his life another fifteen to twenty years.

Even though Emma was told not to rush back she felt the need to be there. She told Olivia to stay home with the children and she'd call her later when there was some progress. The kids missed their mother. With daddy in the hospital all this time, Emma felt it was necessary that Olivia spend some time with them while she could, before Donnie was able to go home. He would need a great deal of help to get around. They lived in a town house apartment and Emma was thinking that he'd never be able to climb stairs when he first came home. She wondered if he should go to her place which was all on one floor, but she knew how much he needed to be with his kids again.

There was plenty of time to make plans for that, she reasoned and sat in the family waiting room, reading a magazine until they let her go in to sit with her son.

Around ten that morning, after the team had done their rounds and examined Donnie, Emma was allowed to go in and sit with him for a short time. She had to put on a gown over her clothes, and booties over her shoes, plastic gloves and a paper mask. She knew the routine.

She stood beside his bed, her eyes flooded with tears of joy that he was still alive and getting stronger. She looked at all the monitors and listened to all the sounds. She watched as his eyelids flicked and fluttered. A nurse had entered the room unnoticed and told Emma, "he's dreaming". She smiled.

"The team said he's doing great. They are talking about removing his breathing tube later today. It's unheard of but they said his lungs seem to be breathing on their own. The whole team is talking about him. His surgery was spot on." She adjusted a few things and left the room as quietly as she had entered.

Emma never even got time to sit down when a doctor and male nurse entered. They explained that she would have to leave for a little while. They were going to do some tests and see if it was safe to remove the breathing tube. He told her she could come back in about an hour.

Emma left the room and walked over to the bin that collected the paper gowns, booties and masks. She almost ran to the elevator and went down through the lobby and outside to the courtyard to call Olivia.

"Liv. They are going to remove his breathing tube. They said he's doing great. Maybe you want to come in. They said they needed an hour. Do you want me to come stay with the kids so you can be here?"

Liv was grateful for the offer. She said she'd try to call the babysitter to come at three so Emma could go back, but she wanted to be there herself when the tube came out.

While watching her grandchildren Emma checked her cell phone for messages. Katie and Jess had both sent her text messages.

First she checked Katie's to find an apology. Nothing big, no details, Just an "I'm sorry for what I said last night, mom."

Next she checked Jessie's message. "Please call me when you are free to talk."

Emma made the call.

"Hi Ma." Jess sounded like she had a terrible cold, stuffy and congested."

"You sound awful baby. Katie told me you've got the flu. Why didn't you tell me?" Emma suspected it was more than the flu.

"Ma it's a long story and I didn't want to bother you. You've got your hands full there with Donnie and Olivia and the kids. We can talk about it later. It's no big deal. I'll be fine. I just wanted to hear about Donnie. Katie had a bad night and she wasn't talking much this morning. So I thought I'd get the details from you."

Emma gave her the details and her voice lifted when she told Jess that they were going to pull the tube out so Donnie could breathe on his own with his new lungs. It was such a big deal. Jessie was very happy or at least she said she was, but Emma noted a sadness in her voice.

"Jessie, honey. What is wrong? I can hear it in your voice. Please tell me."

"Brad got me pregnant, Mom. And I got very sick, morning sickness that lasted all day. Anyway, long story short, he told me to get rid of it. He said if I didn't have an abortion he'd leave me. He didn't want a kid. Whatever. I wouldn't abort it and he left me. Now I find out, he had another girlfriend that he was seeing for the past six months and he was planning on leaving me anyway. I was a mess. I was missing some classes and couldn't work. I was broke. Katie helped me a little. But then I had a miscarriage the day before yesterday. Katie took me to the ER and they checked me out. I'll be fine physically in a few more days, I'm just an emotional wreck, Mom. And I didn't want to burden you with it, way out there. There was nothing you could do." Jess sniffled and blew her nose. She couldn't stop crying.

"Oh my poor Jessie. I am so very sorry baby. I'm never too busy for you, sweetheart. I wish you knew that. If you need money, tell me how much. I can transfer some funds into your account. You get an automatic deposit from my account every month so I know it can be done immediately. It's the least I can do for you honey, until I get home." Emma felt like she had been kicked in the stomach.

"One more thing, Ma. I got kicked out of my apartment. Brad was paying the rent and I didn't know it but he hadn't paid it for three months and I had no money so I was asked to leave. That's why I'm here at Katie's. Can I stay at your house until you get home? Please, Ma? I promise not to make a mess. I'll pay the utilities once I get on my feet. I need to study for finals and I can't do that here with all this mess here and little Ricky yelling and screaming all day. Ma, that kid is a holy terror." She chuckled.

Emma told her of course she could stay at her house and she told her that she'd put some money into her account. They discussed details and Emma hung up feeling a little better. No wonder Katie was drinking. Emma was ready for a drink and it was only noon.

She called Bill. "Do you have time for a quick lunch surrounded by two wild Indians?" She invited him over to Olivia's and he offered to pick up pizza for them and the kids. At least she had time alone with him while the kids played in their rooms upstairs. She told him all about the conversation with Jessie and he shook his head.

"It is always something with our kids. No matter how old they get, we are still their parents and we still come to their rescue when necessary."

Emma said when Donnie gets released she'll stay to help Olivia until he is strong enough for her to leave, so perhaps she'd be home in another five to six weeks. They said their good byes and promised to write and/or call. He wished Donnie the best recovery ever and also promised to get the firemen to empty their pockets into the donation site. Emma was ever grateful.

By three thirty, Emma was on her way back to the hospital since the babysitter had taken over. She had planned to spend the night so there was no rush for either Emma or Olivia to rush home. The babysitter said she had no plans for the next day so she'd stay as long as she was needed. She was a great young lady. Olivia was lucky to have found her. She thanked her lucky stars.

Emma peeked in the glass window at Olivia sitting at Donnie's bedside. When Olivia saw her, she came out so Emma could gown up and go inside. One at a time, they had been told. Then Dr. Tessler happened to come by and said it was okay for them both to be there. They were weaning Donnie off his sleeping meds and he would soon begin to wake up slowly. So Emma joined Liv sitting side by side, watching as Donnie's eyes began to flutter and every so often, he let out a groan of pain.

The first time he started to come to, the monitors began to beep and ring and it was letting the doctors know, it was too soon. Donnie was in distress. His pain was too intense. He needed more rest, so more meds were fed into his IV line.

At five thirty, the two women went down stairs to the cafeteria and got some coffee and a bite to eat. They made their personal phone calls and returned to the room an hour later.

By nine o'clock Donnie began to moan once again and his eyes fluttered then he opened his eyes. He couldn't focus, but he was waking up. Emma signaled one of the nurses who came right away and told the women to hush. She checked his vitals and smiled.

"Hey Donnie. Mom and Liv are both here. How are you feeling?" The nurse spoke in a soft, soothing voice to see if he would respond.

He tried hard to open his eyes but his lids were weighted down with drugs. He did manage a little smile on one side of his face, however, and then he groaned and went back to sleep.

"It's going to take time, ladies. You need to be patient. If you want to go home we can call you if he wakes up. This could take several hours before he is fully awake."

Olivia looked at Emma and Emma looked back and they smiled and sat back down. They were in this for the long haul. When he woke up, they both wanted to be there with him. They took turns dozing in the recliner while the other stood watch.

The sun was starting to come up over the mountains outside his window when Emma shook Olivia and whispered. "Livvy, wake up. I think he's waking up. Liv."

Olivia opened her eyes and sat up straight in her chair, trying to shake the sleep from her head.

"What are you two whispering about?", Donnie croaked with a dry throat and a smile followed by a deep moaning sound.

A nurse noticed the commotion and came rushing into the room to check his vitals. "Well good morning sunshine. It's about time you woke up," the nurse teased. "How are you feeling there young man?"

"I feel like a Mack truck ran over me, then backed up to do it again." They all laughed. He never lost his sense of humor. "I hurt like hell."

"Well we can do something about that, Donovan. But we are very happy to have you back with us here. I'll be back with some nice pain meds but you'll have to go back to sleep a while longer. Okay honey?" She hurried off to get him a cocktail for his IV.

Both Mom and Olivia kissed his cheeks through their paper masks and once again, Donnie drifted off to sleep.

Olivia sat at his bedside while Emma took a walk outside to make some calls. As promised to Bill, she texted Lenny with an update for him to keep posting on his Face Book page that he set up specifically for Donnie's progress.

She phoned Bill and he was just walking through his door at home after his long, overnight flight back, which had been delayed twice before leaving LAX.

"Oh wow, that's great news, Emma. I'm so happy for all of you." He said wearily.

Next she called Jess and got her voice mail so she left her a message. Then it was Katie's turn who answered right away.

"Hi Mom. How's it going?" She sounded like the old Katie.

Emma gave her the news that Donnie woke up and was talking, in a great deal of pain but he was doing as well as could be expected after a surgery of that magnitude.

She inquired about Jess. Katie informed her that Jess was feeling a lot better today and she was at the library studying for exams. She told Emma that Jess' cell phone was with her suitcase. She was going to move later in the day, over to Emma's house.

Emma then inquired, casually, how Katie's husband was,

remembering he hadn't come home after work the last time when they spoke.

Katie chuckled. "Don't be afraid to ask, Mom. He's a jerk at times, but he's fine. He had a few too many beers the other night, got into his pickup truck to drive home and fell asleep before he turned on the ignition. After he slept a few hours, he came home all apologies. I was glad he was safe and didn't drive drunk. I'll punish him somehow, but for now, all is fine. Thanks for asking, Mom. Sorry I was such a shit that night. I was just down and out and pissed off."

"Tell it like it is, My Katie girl. You do have a way with words," Emma chuckled into the phone.

Katie was forgiven for her attitude but the things she said still wrung strong in Emma's head. Her daughter said she was always too busy with Donnie to take care of the girls. It was an accusation that Emma could not forget. It would have to be addressed when she got home and could talk to both her daughters in person.

Chapter 17

On day #3 Emma stood outside of the glass walls of Donnie's room while his wife and a nurse were inside with him. Lenny was with Emma taking a video with his iPhone. The nurse was assisting Donnie to help him stand up for the first time since surgery.

He was weak and a little apprehensive. He still had some heavy duty pains across his chest at the sight of his incision. But his breathing was all on his own; no oxygen for the first time in over a year.

He was sitting at the side of the bed, making small talk with his wife and the nurse, always kidding around.

"You want me to stand up and walk to the chair, right? Are you kidding me? That must be six miles away." The chair was only 4 steps from his bed. They all chuckled.

"Come on, Donnie, just push yourself forward and stand," the nurse instructed, standing close by his side ready to assist.

"Oh," remarked Donnie. "You want me to do this *now?* " Again, giggles from the two women.

The tears of happiness gathered as puddles in Emma's eyes. Three days after a double lung transplant and her son was kidding around and about to take his first steps. Lenny was getting it all in pictures and video. He would use this for a documentary one day. He was going to make Donnie famous. He'd show how courageous he is.

Donnie stood still for a minute, holding on to the nurse's arm.

"One step at a time Donnie; just go slow." Olivia was urging him forward.

"That's easy for you to say, Liv." He turned and gave her one of his handsome smiles. He was a good looking man, even with a week's growth of whiskers.

Donnie took one step, two, then three and looked at the nurse as his wobbly legs were about to give out. "How do I turn around?" He was beginning to waiver.

Olivia to the rescue. She moved the chair, placing it directly behind him. Donnie eased into the chair with both of their help.

"Bless you, Livvy. I knew I married you for something." She leaned over and kissed him through her paper mask.

"I haven't heard him talk this much in months," Emma whispered to Lenny who was standing beside her, mesmerized at what he just witnessed.

Seeing his mother through the glass wall, he waved. "Hi Ma. I'm going to run a marathon next year. Mark it down on the calendar. I'll be running marathons before you know it. I love you, Ma." He threw her a kiss in the air and that did it. The dam broke and the tears fell from her eyes.

Lenny had captured it all. He then kissed Emma's forehead and said he'd call her later and he was gone to do some creative writing.

Emma left Olivia to sit with her husband a few minutes then help him back to bed where he would crash and burn with pain meds for the next three hours. Walking that first time after such trauma from surgery is exhausting. Emma went back to Olivia's house to set the babysitter free. She had been a Godsend, filling in at odd hours of the day and night.

Emma got the children settled down for a little nap after lunch.

She needed some time alone; some peaceful time to think and digest all that had happened the past three days. Then she decided to call Jessie to see how she was doing.

Jessie's phone went directly to voice mail. Then almost instantly, Emma received a text from her saying that Jess was at the library doing some research with her phone off but she felt it vibrate. She told her mother that she'd call her when she got home; home to Emma's house, where she was now living comfortably.

She called Katie and had a delightful chat with her. She told her about Donnie taking his first steps and Katie told her about the ultra sound she had done the day before. Katie was going to have a sister for little Ricky to play with. She was ecstatic.

Emma made herself a cup of tea and picked up her long forgotten book that she had started a week prior. She just got comfy on the sofa, with her legs folded up on the cushions when her cell phone rang. Jessie.

"How come you are not in class Jess?" Her mother questioned.

"It's a crazy week, Mom. We are having final exams all week

and they are scheduled at all different times, so when I'm not in class taking an exam, I'm at the library studying for the next exam."

Emma was confused. "Jess, why are you taking final exams in September?"

Jessie laughed. "Oh Mom. How soon we forget. Don't you remember that I got accepted into this accelerated nursing program? I had to go to classes all through the summer months in order to graduate early. We are having exams now, then we go three more months with more exams, the real final ones. If we pass we graduate in January instead of having to go 'til May. I know you've been so preoccupied with Donnie. I guess you don't remember." Jessie sounded disappointed in her mother's lack of understanding how hard it had been on Jess to get accepted into this program and even harder staying in it. It was compact and complicated and very time consuming. She could only work three or four nights in order to study and keep her grades up, thus her weak finances.

"I'm sorry, Jessie. I guess I didn't realize the pressure you were under. How are your grades?"

"I'm doing awesome, Mom. I love it. But Brad kept trying to derail me, wanting me to blow off class and go places with him. It was one reason why we weren't getting along. He didn't understand how much this means to me. I'm going to be an RN, Mom. And then I can earn good money while helping people. I want this so bad. I guess I was working so hard at it that I had forgotten to take my birth control pills for several days. Stupid me. When I realized that I was pregnant, I was devastated. I didn't know what I was going to do and then I got sick with the pregnancy which complicated things even more. I turned to Katie and she helped me through it. If you had been home here, Ma, I would have told you, honest, but I didn't want to burden you while you were out there."

Emma understood but felt badly that she wasn't available for her first born child in her time of need. She apologized for not being there for her.

"No biggie, Ma. God took care of things I couldn't, like He did for Donnie." Jess always had a way with words to make people feel better. Emma was glad that she had given religion to her children, not that she was a devout Catholic or anything however, having faith in a greater power made a difficult life a little bit easier; you didn't feel quite so alone when you knew you had a God to help get you through your day.

Chapter 18

Each day Donnie accomplished something new and broke
more records on his road to recovery. There was no need for Olivia
and Emma to do round the clock shifts anymore, Donnie was on his
way back to join the living once again. They found a routine that
worked for both of them and they were able to give the kids more
personal time.

On the fifth day after his surgery, Olivia was allowed to bring
the children in for a visit. It was a joyous occasion. Donnie had been a
little worried that one of them would jump on his sore chest but Olivia
had given them stern precautions. She sat them both down before they
entered the hospital and explained all about daddy's surgery.

The children could sit on daddy's bed but they were told not to
get too close to him. They could throw him kisses from behind their
paper clothes and masks. Children breed germs and rejection is the
enemy for a post transplant patient, so they weren't allowed to get too
close, Olivia warned them.

"Daddy," asked little Billy. "If your staples fall out, will you fall apart?" He was so serious and so curious. Mom and Daddy both laughed.

"I guess I didn't explain it quite right, huh?" Liv said to Donnie.

"No honey. Daddy won't fall apart. They'd just have to put new ones in." Donnie rubbed the top of his son's head. He was feeling very emotional but all of a sudden, he also felt weary and needed to rest.

Olivia saw it in his face and told the kids it was time to go. Daddy will be coming home before you know it, she told them. They squealed with delight. All the way home in the car they chanted, "Daddy's coming home. Daddy's coming home."

One week after his surgery, walking down the hall with his pole attached, he said that he just wished he could go outside to breathe some fresh air. He had been in the hospital over a month without ever being able to go outside.

Olivia went to the nurse and inquired if that was possible. The nurse said she'd contact Dr. Tessler and ask if it was possible or too soon. "We don't want him having a relapse. He's pushing hard and going a little too fast, in my opinion. He needs time to heal and get stronger."

By the time the doctor got back to the nurse with his answer, Donnie was sound asleep in his bed. The nurse came into the room and told Olivia that if the weather was nice the following day, they would make arrangements to wheel him outside for a short time. Olivia thanked her and smiled. She'd have a nice bit of news for her husband when he woke up. He'd be pleased.

It was a picture perfect day in the mid seventies. There was hardly a cloud in the blue sky. They covered Donnie in paper garments from head to toe. The last thing they wanted was for him to be exposed to someone outside who was sick or had a cold. They helped him into a wheel chair and the nurse connected his IV pole to the chair. They put a light blanket over his legs to prevent him from getting a chill.

Emma was waiting in the lobby downstairs when they came out of the elevator, and Olivia at his side, holding his hand. Donnie was almost giddy with the idea of going out doors for the first time.

The double doors opened wide to let him exit the building and he was pushed over to the left side where there were benches for people to sit and relax. The nurse put his chair in place at the end of the bench, locked it in place and straightened his blanket, made sure he was comfortable. His wife and his mother waited patiently for the nurse to finish fussing with him, then she left, saying she'd return in twenty minutes. The women sat on the bench and they were all silent for a very long time, taking in the beauty all around them.

Donnie took several deep breaths as tears slid down his cheeks. "I'd forgotten how good it felt to breathe fresh air," he cried. He wiped his face with the blanket.

A nurse from the eighth floor was on her way in to work and she saw Donnie sitting there. She ran over to him, screaming with delight. "Look at you. Oh my good God almighty. A week ago you could barely talk and now you are sitting outside. I am so happy for you Donnie. God bless you honey." Then she turned to shake hands with Olivia and Emma, knowing better than to touch Donnie, she threw him a kiss as she hurried off inside the building.

A young man was passing between buildings and he too came over to say hello to Donnie. He was a therapist who worked on Donnie two days a week for several weeks.

"Look at the good color in your face, young man. You look so fine." He said in his Jamaican accent. "I wish you well."

Other people waved and said hello and then he saw one of his fellow CFers, being wheeled outside. "That's Jason. He had his transplant three weeks ago." They waved to one another. Jason still looked weak and unstable. Donnie was so much stronger.

"Jason was on the list for over a year. He hasn't left this hospital since last May. He is very grateful to still be alive. I never thought he'd live long enough to get it done."

Two weeks and two days after his surgery, Donnie broke all records and he walked out of the hospital to go home.

He had a picc line for the IV medication that he would need to have round the clock for the next several weeks. He would need to go to outpatient care once a week for several weeks, getting blood work done and chest exrays. Rejection was something that would have to be carefully monitored. It could happen at any time but the first three months were critical.

The house had to be spotless, free of germs, so Emma hired a professional cleaning crew to go through the house and clean everything that Donnie would come in contact with. They put clean new sheets on the bed. Emma replaced all of the scatter rugs with new ones. The children would not go to pre-school for a few weeks to avoid coming in contact with other children who might have a virus or a cold.

Emma offered her place for Donnie to stay for a while but he refused, wanting to sleep in his own bed with his wife and be near his kids. Being around the kids made him nervous but they'd all learn to adjust. Emma said she would take the kids over night for a few nights, until Donnie got adjusted and settled in. He agreed to that arrangement as long as he could be with them during the day.

The doctor suggested that he go to a post transplant rehab apartment not too far from the hospital, just for a month or two, but Donnie rejected that idea. He had lived apart from his family for so long already, he wanted to get back to some form of normalcy. It had been so hard on his wife, dealing with the kids and him being away in the hospital. The doctor said they would see how things worked out with him at home but if there were any complications, he had to promise to go into the rehab housing. So Donnie knew he had to follow the rules precisely in order to be able to stay at home. It wasn't easy with two small children living in the house but they did their best. Olivia was so nervous she was beginning to upset the children by yelling at them to be quiet and let daddy sleep or no running in the house, don't jump on your father.

One day little Beth looked at her mother and said "Mommy. Did you forget that we are just little kids?" And Liv and Donnie both laughed.

Donnie said, "Yeah Mommy. They're just little kids. Did you forget?"

Olivia stopped her cleaning for just a minute and went to her children, bending down and giving them a group hug. "Yes babies. I guess I did forget that. But we must be so careful to take good care of daddy so he doesn't get sick again and have to go back into the hospital. So I need you little kids to act like BIG kids and help mommy take good care of daddy. Can you do that for me please?" they both agreed simultaneously.

Later on, when Mommy and Daddy were together and the children were up taking their naps, Donnie reached out and grabbed Olivia's arm and pulled her down next to him on the sofa. He kissed her and put his arm around her. She rested her head on his shoulder.

"Thank you for trying so hard and taking such good care of me. I don't thank you enough, and by the way, that was a good save with the kids earlier. Nice come back." He kissed her again. "Just sit here with me for just a few minutes. The germs can wait to be extinguished." He held her in his arms and she loved having him home again.

A few days later, Emma went over to visit with her son and his family and Olivia had just put the two children down for a short nap. They had been rambunctious all day. She wanted time to relax and read for a while so Emma asked Donnie if he wanted to go for a little walk. There was an ice cream store two blocks away, she offered to buy him an ice cream sundae. She realized Olivia needed some alone time.

"You're on, Mom. But only if you will help me eat it."

It was a lovely day and they took their time but he walked the quarter mile up and back without any effort at all. His breathing was as normal as Emma's.

"What are you smiling about, Ma?" Donnie asked her as they rounded the corner to home.

"I'm listening to you breathe like a normal person, no huffing and puffing, no coughing. You talk as you walk. I can't believe how well you are doing, just weeks after that tremendous surgery. God must have more plans ahead for you, Donnie."

"I've thought of that myself, Ma. Not today, before, when he kept me alive to get this transplant. I asked Him, how come you don't want me back yet, Lord? Do you have something left for me to do here? I guess he wants me to help Olivia raise those two brats."

Donnie laughed out loud. He was in such a great mood, so happy to be alive, feeling so blessed.

The following week Olivia drove Donnie to the lab at six thirty in the morning. The children slept over Nana's house for her to babysit while Donnie went for his appointments with the blood lab and radiology for his chest exray. They would then go back home to rest and have an early lunch followed by a return trip to the hospital to meet with his doctor for the lab results. It was an exhausting day for them but it was something they would have to do every Thursday for many weeks to come.

After the doctor's appointment Donnie and Olivia went to Emma's place to pick up the children. Donnie walked inside and sat down on the sofa. He had never been inside this rented condo. He was in the hospital when she moved in temporarily.

"Nice place Mom." He said, glancing around at her space. "Mom, you look beat. Did the kids misbehave?" Donnie had told her about what Beth said to Olivia.

"No, they didn't misbehave, Donnie but they are 'just little kids' with a lot of pent up energy. I know now why God gives babies only to young women." They all laughed.

"So how did you make out? Any idea when you will begin rehab therapy?" Emma asked her son.

"Well we had nothing but good news today, Ma. All my tests are good. They did have to adjust some of my meds because my potassium was low and I'm getting leg cramps, but other than that, it was all good. Oh, and guess what? He said I don't need therapy. He said if I can climb the stairs in my townhouse, go for a half mile walk with you and deal with two young children then I'm as good as it gets. No rehab."

Emma clapped her hands at the great news.

"We were talking on the way home, Mom." Olivia spoke up. "You've been here quite a while and we know it all costs money. Now that we have that wonderful donation site to help us financially, I can put the kids back into day care full time and since Donnie won't need rehab three times a week like we expected, I think I'll be able to take care of him. The doctors are amazed at his progress; they can't believe how strong he is already."

"Oh," Emma replied. "So you are telling me to go the hell home, are you?" She smiled. "I'm kidding. I think that's wonderful news. I was going to have to pay another month's rent in advance on Monday but if you think it's safe to leave, I wouldn't mind going home to my own bed and checking on my two forsaken daughters."

They talked about it for a few minutes then Liv rounded up the kids and their belongings and headed for home. Emma handed Olivia a casserole she had made for them for dinner so she wouldn't have to cook after such a long day.

"I love you Mom. I'm going to miss you." Olivia hugged her tight.

Donnie too gave her a hug and kiss on the cheek as he went out the door.

Emma sat down in the living room chair and let her head fall back. She was so glad that she had been able to be here for all of this but she would also be very happy to get home, so see her other kids and her grandson and to help Katie when she has her baby girl. And yes, to see Bill again. With that thought, she smiled and reached for her phone to call him.

"I'm coming home next week Bill. I can't believe how well he's doing."

Chapter 19

Bill picked Emma up at Logan airport the day after Halloween on Saturday, November 1st. She had a direct flight on JetBlue that lasted five and a half hours. She was tired and hungry. She had packed some snacks to have on the plane with the free beverage service but that didn't go very far. She had a seven a.m. flight so she arrived by shuttle service at five ten to check her luggage and get through the endless security at LAX, even at that ungodly hour. She had coffee and a muffin while she waited to board. Even though it was just four in the afternoon, Boston time, it was past lunch time for her stomach and it was growling by the time she met Bill outside of the terminal.

"So good of you to pick me up Billy. I could have taken a shuttle to Braintree to save you some time of coming in here at this hour" Emma's exhaustion was showing.

"It's Saturday, Emma. The traffic isn't nearly as bad as during the week at rush hour. Are you hungry? Do you want to stop for a bite to eat before we go home?"

"I'm famished, Bill. I could eat a whole cow right now," she smiled at him.

They got off the highway half way home, in Braintree. There were several chain restaurants right off route 3. They grabbed a quick bite to eat and got right back on the road home. It had been a long time since Emma was home and she was anxious. She missed her little cottage by the beach. She smiled thinking about going home, as they rode in silence, once her tummy was full from fish and chips, New England style.

Bill pulled into Emma's driveway in Yarmouth. He had never been to her house and he was curious to see it. Jessie's car was in the driveway. Emma had almost forgotten that her daughter had moved in while she was gone. Part of her wished she could go inside alone to show Bill around, have some privacy, but another part of her was happy to be greeted by her daughter. She should have texted her to let her know what time she'd be getting in, but she last texted Jess from Los Angeles saying that she was ready to board the plane, 'see you later'.

Emma opened the door, carrying her pocketbook and carry-on

luggage. Bill followed her, wheeling her big suitcase.

"Jessie. I'm home honey. Jess, where are you?" Emma called out. The house was not very big so where could her daughter be hiding? Maybe in the bathroom or her bedroom.

Emma put her pocketbook and small suitcase on the table and went to see where her daughter was, when there was no response.

"She's not here," Emma told him as she returned to the kitchen. "Here, let me take that, have a look around. I'm sorry the place is such a mess." Emma was embarrassed at the way Jessie left the house, knowing that she was coming home today with Bill. It made her angry and there would be words said when Jess came back.

"She must have gone for a run or for a walk on the beach. She loves to run, but I can't believe she'd go out leaving the place like this knowing I was coming home. I'm pissed." Emma told Bill just how she felt.

"Don't worry about the mess, Emma. You are finally home. You'll have it cleaned up in no time, if I know you." He pulled her into a warm hug.

Emma showed him around, turning on lights as she went. She looked at the fireplace and saw the end of some wood still burning. How could Jess have gone out and left a fire burning? She wondered. She added some crumpled up newspaper that was in a basket beside the hearth, added a little kindling and a log and the fire reignited, casting a warm glow in the living room.

There was dust on the end tables and papers that looked like research papers strewn everywhere. Jessie must have been studying in here before she went out. Was she that busy with school and work that she couldn't have dusted in what looked like weeks?

The trash barrels in the kitchen and bathroom were both overflowing and needed to be emptied. As Emma walked through her house, she got more and more angry with her daughter. How could she live like this, and knowing I was coming home today?

"Wouldn't you think she'd have cleaned up, just a little bit?" She asked Bill as she shook her head. Her face was flushed with disappointment in her first born child.

"Some welcome home this is." She was fit to be tied.

Bill knew Emma was tired and that she was going to confront her daughter the minute the young lady came through that door and he didn't want to be there when that happened, so he decided it was a good time to say good bye and leave. Emma thanked him for the ride and her lunch. He told her that he'd call her the following day and he was out the door.

After Emma unpacked her two suitcases and Jessie still hadn't returned, she started to get concerned. Then she heard a text message come into her phone. She reached for it and saw that it was from Donnie. "Are you home yet?" Emma smiled and returned his text, "yep, safe and sound".

Next she called Katie to tell her that she was home and to ask her if she knew where Jessie could be.

"You wouldn't believe the mess in this place. I could clobber that girl," Emma complained to her younger daughter, who laughed.

"Mom, you know Jess is a slob. Did you ever go to her apartment? Oh my God, she has no clue how to keep a clean house."

"But Katie, she knew I was coming home and she went out, no

note, a fire burning in the fireplace and my beautiful home is trashed with dust and overflowing rubbish. Wait 'til I get my hands on her." Katie laughed again.

"But where could she be, Katie? Her car is in the driveway. I've been home over an hour."

Katie said if she heard from her that she'd call. They hung up and Emma threw on a shawl that Jess had hanging from a hook near the back door. Emma wondered if she had gone out without a jacket? The nights were cold. She took a flashlight and walked down to the beach and looked around. Not a soul in sight. She called Jessie's name but there was no reply. Where had she gone? It was after eight o'clock.

Emma poured herself a half glass of red wine, emptying the bottle, the only thing left in the house to drink besides tea and coffee. There had been about a half dozen bottles of wine when she locked up the house to fly to California in early September. If Jess was going to continue to live here there would be some rules set down, that was for sure.

At ten past eight, her cell phone rang. It was Katie.

"Mom, Jess is here. You can stop worrying."

"Oh thank heavens. Where the hell was she and why is she there?"

Katie explained that Brad showed up at her door when she was studying and he was drunk. She did not want to let him inside so she stepped out into the driveway to talk to him. He said he was sorry. He didn't know she lost the baby. He wanted her to take him back. Apparently his new girlfriend kicked him out and he had no place to stay. Anyway, she got into his car with him to talk because she was getting cold and he took off so they could go someplace to talk. And of course, he drove to a bar down the street.

"She didn't have her cell phone on her to call and he got drunker and they had a big fight. She had no money on her so some friend at the bar drove her to my house. She left Brad there. She was ticked but she didn't want to go to your house like this, knowing you just got home. She's a bit drunk too, so she's sleeping it off on my couch. I'll bring her home in the morning. Get some rest, Ma."

No matter how old your children are, they will always be your children. You will always worry about them and love them unconditionally.

Emma went to bed once the fire burned itself out and she slept like a baby in her own bed for the first time in months. It was good to be home even if it was eventful.

Chapter 20

November 6th, Donnie was scheduled to have his second

Bronchoscopy, or Bronc. A **Bronchoscopy** is the procedure that

allows a doctor to look at your airway through a thin viewing

instrument called a **bronchoscope**. During a bronchoscopy, the doctor

will examine the throat, larynx, trachea, and lower airways. Donnie

had his first Bronc three weeks after his surgery. He will have them on

a regular basis to check for rejection and/or infection. It is done as an

outpatient service but takes several hours for the prep, anesthesia and

recovery. It makes for a very long day.

It was a routine that Donnie was going to have to get used to

but Emma sensed he seemed nervous about having it done on

Thursday.

"What seems to be the problem, Donnie? Are you feeling

okay?" Mom asked.

He told her the past few days he had been coughing more than

he had been since the surgery and he was a little more congested.

Rejection and Infection were very real fears after a transplant operation.

In the meantime, back on Cape Cod Jessie had taken all of her exams and had a few days off before her next semester began. To make up for the mess her mother came home to, she stayed around the house to help Emma clean. They had their little chat; or rather Jess listened while Emma spoke, setting down the ground rules. When Mom started a conversation with "Jessica Marie", her daughter knew that she was in big trouble. The agreement was that Jessie could stay there, rent free, until she finished school. After she graduated and the holidays were behind them, she would need to look for a place to rent and get a full time job. Jess agreed that was more than fair. She would save up the money she was making as a bartender for a deposit. Emma wanted her privacy back and her home to herself. She wanted to be able to entertain Bill without her daughter coming and going at all hours of the day and night. Jess was quickly approaching forty years old. She might never be a good house keeper but while she lived in Emma's house, she would pick up and clean up after herself and share the duties around the house, like taking out the rubbish on collection day. She didn't need to be living with her mother. Her taste in the men she chose for relationships had not been wise choices. She would have to stand on her own two feet and take care of herself. Hopefully her nursing career would work out. Jess was already looking at help wanted ads for nurses.

Wednesday evening Emma got a text from Donnie.

"I'm in the hospital. Just a precautionary measure. I'll be here to have the bronc tomorrow. They wanted to start me on IV meds due to my cough." Emma thought it was best to be safe rather than sorry. She said a silent prayer for her son.

Friday he called her. "I'm in early stages of rejection so they've vamped up my antibiotics and added steroids and an anti-fungal medication. I'll be here for a few more days."

It scared Emma when he said "rejection". It was almost like that horrible word "Incurable". But it happens and they were ready to combat it. They'd just have to wait and see and hope and pray for the best.

Due to the living arrangements, Emma found herself driving over the Sagamore Bridge on her way to Plymouth more and more often. She and Bill were spending a great deal of time together. Even though it was recently renovated, his house needed some updating and some female touches. He had a cleaning service come in once a month to do the necessary upkeep but the house needed some TLC. There were just blinds on the windows, no curtains or valances. Only blankets on the beds, no quilts or bedspreads. Comfortable living but no finishing touches since Maddie had died. His mother had been old school and never wanted to ask him for money to replace things once they wore out.

Thanksgiving was approaching and Emma said she'd like to do something with the families. But his house was not ideally suited for it and hers was too small. They were sitting on his living room sofa, side by side, sipping on white wine and discussing the possibilities.

"Emma." He started a new thought. "What are we waiting for?"

She looked him square in the eye. "I don't know what you mean? Are you talking about Thanksgiving or something else?"

"I'm talking about us, Emma, and you know damn well what I'm talking about. I see that gleam in your eye and the corners of your mouth in an almost-smile. I'm asking you what are we waiting for? We love each other. We have for years. We need to decide where we are going to live when we get married, Emma. Why are we waiting to get married? Emma let's get married. Now. I want to get married now, before the damn holidays." He pulled her closer and kissed her. "Will you marry me, Emma?"

He pulled back to look at her, waiting for her answer.

Little by little, as she sat silent contemplating his question, her 'almost smile' became a full smile. She pulled him back into her embrace and kissed him hard.

"Yes, you silly boy. I WILL marry you. Now. I don't care where we live as long as we live together. Yes, Bill. Let's get married before the holiday."

He jumped to his feet, pulling her up off the couch. He picked her up into his arms like she was feather weight and carried her into his bed as she laughed and giggled all the way down the hall.

The following Friday they were married at City Hall, just the two of them. They didn't want any one with them. They didn't want any fuss. After exchanging their vows they went out to dinner at the harbor and spent their wedding night in a hotel. They had room service in bed the next morning and drank Mimosa's and made love until noon when they had to rush to check out.

On the drive back to his house Emma giggled. "I can't believe we are actually married. Wait until we tell the kids. They'll think we're crazy."

"I think we are crazy for not doing this thirty years ago." He said with a smile.

"Now we really need to concentrate on where we are going to live, Bill. Really. I think we need a place of our own; not your house or mine. What do you think?"

"Whatever you want, Mrs. Jeffers. You are a very shrewd woman and I agree with you completely. We need a place of our own.

Where shall it be? Plymouth or on the Cape? Or someplace else?"

They threw out ideas and talked about it and decided to contact someone in a real estate office, just to see what was available. One thing that Bill said which made a lot of sense was that she should keep her place on the beach. The property values had escalated since she bought it. Jessie could pay rent when she got a full time nursing job and stay right there if she wanted to. It was a lovely spot. If Jess moved out, she could rent it to summer residents. It was a good plan. He would definitely put his house up for sale and since he no longer had a mortgage on it, he'd get a chunk of change to put down on a new place for them. All they had to do was find that place.

A friend of Bill's sold real estate so they called him and made an appointment to sit down and talk to him about places that they might be interested in seeing. An hour later, they were taking a ride to check out a new development that Mike told him about. It was almost all sold out so now they were beginning to sell the model homes furnished and professionally decorated. A notice had just gone out to the local realtors that same day so he urged Bill to check it out and see if they liked the location and he told them to go through the models. They were open from eleven to four daily.

The development consisted of about sixty new homes with five different basic models. It was in the part of Plymouth they called Manomet. It was up on a bluff that overlooked Plymouth harbor, it was a lovely location, only about fifteen minutes from the Sagamore Bridge that went to Cape Cod, and only ten minutes to the highway that led into Boston. They both agreed it was a good location and a real nice setting.

They toured 3 of the homes before being captured by an on-site realtor. She explained some things to them about the area but having lived in Plymouth most of his adult life, Bill was familiar with the area. What he didn't know was the builder was planning on building a community club house with an Olympic sized pool now that most of the lots were sold. The builder's son was already living in one of the homes there. Three other families had already moved in as well while the other homes were still being built. That was a good thing to know. It spoke well about the quality of the homes.

After informing the woman that they were already working with a realtor, they moved on to view the fourth model. The instant Emma walked into the front to back split she broke out into a huge smile. They liked the last model, the split entry, but she liked this style even more.

To the left of the front entrance was a good sized fireplaced living room with five steps up to the bed and bath level. The master bedroom was quite large and bright with two windows to let in the sunlight. It had its own master bathroom that was also roomy. There were two other bedrooms but they had one set up as a study or a den, which would be perfect for Emma to use as an office to do her bookkeeping. There was another full bathroom between the two rooms.

They walked down the stairs and went into the kitchen-dining room area which was to the right of the front door. There was granite counter tops and the best of appliances in stainless steel. The dining area had a full table with six chairs and a small hutch that held designer plates in yellow and orange. She loved the colorful décor and the openness of the house.

From the dining room, you go down about another six stairs and to the left was a finished recreation room, complete with a sixty inch flat screen television and a small bar with three stools set up in the corner. There were sliding glass doors to a walk out patio and a magnificent view of the water far below. It was breath-taking. The furnace, laundry area and store room to the right of the staircase occupied the rest of the lower level of the house. It too had its own entry out to the back yard.

On the other side of the kitchen was a small open breezeway that could be enclosed at some future date if desired. It led to the over sized two car garage.

There was literature on the kitchen table giving all the details about the heating system and central air and vacuuming systems. And the price, which was a bit more than they wanted to spend, but of course, all was negotiable.

"I don't even have to ask you. I can see it in your expression. You love it, don't you?" Bill reached for his cell phone to call Mike, the realtor friend.

"Make me an offer," Mike said to him after a short discussion. "I'll present it to the builder today."

On their way back to Bill's house, Emma said "I doubt that he'll accept our offer. He'll probably counter offer, don't ya think so?" Bill agreed so they discussed the most they could afford to pay for that house.

"I really love it. It's so unique. And I love the view. We could screen in part of that patio or just install retractable awnings maybe." Emma started to day dream about living in that house.

Early that evening Mike called Bill back to inform him that the builder had been given several offers today regarding the models. He needed a few days to go over them and see what he was going to do.

"I don't know if any other offer was made for that particular home however, so we'll just have to sit tight and wait for his reply."

And while they waited, Emma was trying to find a place for Thanksgiving dinner. She didn't want to go to just any restaurant for a few slices of turkey, potato and a vegetable. She was looking for something more traditional. And then she found it.

"Look at this ad, Billy. It's at the Inn at Sandwich. It says a Traditional Family Style sit down dinner served at your table with free refills, only twenty nine dollars per person."

They decided to go to the Inn on Sunday for brunch, to check out the place and get all the details. If they liked it, they would make reservations. There would be his daughter, Lucy with her husband Scott and four year old, Molly. There would be Jessie, Katie, her husband Joe and three year old Ricky. And Bill and Emma. Nine people. They must have a children's price for the kids, Emma said out loud.

"Too bad Donnie can't be here and Charlie." With the thought of Donnie, Emma walked into another room while texting him to ask what he had planned to do for turkey day. She put her phone down on the coffee table and picked up the paper that had more ads, just to make sure she didn't miss anything else that sounded as good.

Her cell dinged with an incoming text from her son. She read it and smiled.

"Donnie bought a twenty one pound turkey so he's cooking, and they invited Charlie and Lenny to dinner, and they are going. That is so cool. They'll be together."

"How is Donnie feeling now that they have the rejection under control?" Bill asked. Emma explained that his meds were creating havoc with his sleeping and he woke often with leg cramps but other than that, he was doing great.

On their way to brunch Sunday morning, they stopped by the model homes again, just to get another look and they were convinced, they wanted this house. Bill would give Mike a listing on his own house to sell if the builder accepted their offer.

As they were about to get into their car, they noticed a young man down the street raking the leaves in his front yard.

"Isn't that the house the woman realtor told us belonged to the builder's son?" Emma asked Bill. "Let's go talk to him, be neighborly," she joked. "It can't hurt."

So they crossed the street and went down the hill to meet the man out front.

"Hello. My name is Bill. This is my wife Emma." Bill reached out his hand to shake. He was certain the other man must be tired of meeting new people who were just kicking tires, looking at the open houses.

They talked for a while and Bill told him that they put an offer in on Model #4.

"That's a different style house. You either love it or hate it," the man said. "My name is Tim Walker Junior. Say, you look awfully familiar. What did you say your name was?"

"Bill. Bill Jeffers."

"Oh, you were a fireman in town, right? I went to school with Charlie. I've been to your house as a kid, in fact. I dated your daughter a few times, until she met Scott Dowd. Then I was chopped liver." He laughed. "Small damn world."

"Hey, my pop is coming over a little later. My mother made pot roast for dinner last night and she's sending us the left over's so my wife, Sally, won't have to cook when she gets home from work.

She's a nurse at Jordan Hospital." In one sentence he told his life's story. Sally kept telling him that he talks too much.

"I'll ask him if he is considering your offer and I'll give him a little push. It would be nice to have a fireman in the neighborhood, even if you are retired." Tim had a big friendly smile. He was a nice young man.

"Do you work for your father, Tim?" Emma inquired.

"No ma'am. I tried that a long time ago. Father and Son don't always mix well. I'm a paramedic. That's how I met Sally. We're not really married yet, but we've set the date for next June. We've lived together for years though so people think we're married. She wanted to get settled and have her own house before we got married. It took us a while, but we're doing okay. She wants to try to have a baby now. Oh boy. Here I go again. Running my mouth." They all chuckled and said their good byes.

On their way home from brunch, after they made their Thanksgiving reservations for the family, Bill's cell phone rang. It was Mike.

"Walker took your offer, didn't even dicker. You've got the house, Billy boy."

Chapter 21

On Thanksgiving, the family gathered around the large table at the Inn. Once everyone had a drink in front of them Bill used his spoon to clang the side of his water glass while holding his glass of wine up in front of him.

"I have an announcement to make and then we shall have a toast." Everyone became very still and silent. "Two weeks ago Emma and I did something we should have done thirty years ago. We got married." He paused and smiled and kissed Emma's hand. She had not put on the wedding ring he bought her until today. She wore it proudly. The kids were flabbergasted that they had no idea.

"Then on Monday we signed papers to buy a new house and I put my house up for sale. We will be living in Manomet." Again, more aahhs and ooohhhs. "Jessie, you can stay in your mother's house as prearranged until you get a job. Then you can make a decision to rent it from her, or move out and we'll rent it seasonally. Any questions?" They all began to talk at once and Bill and Emma just laughed. They expected that.

Bill raised his glass looking at his wife and said "To us" and they all toasted to their parents' happiness. They took pictures with their phones and then called Donnie on Face Time and to tell their two sons of the great news. They in turn toasted the happy couple. It was a wonderful day of celebration.

And right on queue the servers showed up at tableside with platters of turkey, both white and dark meat, and bowls of stuffing, potatoes, green bean Almondine and candied yams. It was a feast fit for the King's family. When the bowls got low, they were immediately replenished with hot vegetables. They never even finished all of the turkey on the two platters. And then they got their choice of dessert; pumpkin pie ala mode, blueberry pie, caramel custard pudding or ice cream.

The following day Lucy called her father and asked if she could stop by to speak

to him. She and Scott had sat up talking half the night. Lucy wanted to buy her family home; the home her mother and grandmother both died in; the home she was raised in.

That put Bill on the spot. He was looking for a nice full sale to put down on their new house but how could he charge his only daughter that amount of money? Her husband was Bill's foreman so Bill knew how much he made and it wasn't enough to get a mortgage to buy the house for the amount Bill had it listed for sale. Plus he'd have to pay his friend, Mike, a commission. Bill didn't know what to say. He tried to explain how he felt and Lucy began to cry.

"It's our family home dad. You can't just sell it. I love that house."

"But Lucy, it needs new appliances and updating," he tried to reason with her.

"Dad, Scott knows that, did you forget that he works for you doing just that kind of work? He helped you when you renovated it five years ago. He knows what it needs."

"But it all costs money, Lucy and its money I don't want to sink into this house. I need the sale to go through at the price or near the price I am asking. As it is, Mike is only taking half of his normal commission."

"Dad. I am pregnant again. I'm going to have another baby. The house we are renting is only two bedrooms, it's going to be too small. I can work right up until I have the baby since I have a sit down job. I get six weeks of maternity leave and then I'll go back to work. Dad, we need to find another place to live and we've been saving to buy a house of our own. You know that. Please work with us. If we can get bank financing, will you sell us the house? I'm not asking you to reduce your price. You can help Scott do some of the renovations on weekends." She pleaded with her father.

"Okay, fine, Lucy. If you kids can get financed, I'll sell you the house." Bill didn't think for a minute that they would qualify but if they wanted to risk it, he had to let them try. Forty days later, they got bank financed and they signed an agreement. Emma convinced Bill to drop the price and he gave his foreman an increase in his salary, to help them make their payments to the bank.

Chapter 22

Emma was at her house on the Cape, packing up some things she wanted to take with her when they moved into their new house in mid December. They would be in it for Christmas. It was a hectic time of year. She had to leave things for Jessie, keeping the house fully furnished complete with dishes and pots and pans and bed linens and such. They would take some furnishings from Bill's house, but he too was going to leave a lot for his daughter and her family. It was a good thing they bought a *furnished* model home. But they still had to buy bedding and towels and cookware and such. It would be so nice to start out with fresh new things. It was definitely a new beginning for them.

Emma sat down at her kitchen table to catch her breath from packing knick knacks when her cell phone rang. It was Donnie.

"Hi Mom. I was just thinking about you so I thought I'd give you a call." It did Emma's heart good to have him call her. They had gone on for so many years of just texting because he had such a hard time talking while trying to breathe without coughing.

"I've been sitting at my desk, catching up on bills and seeing what we've got left in the bank. The donation site has pretty much dried up but it was a godsend. I don't know how we would have managed without the help of all those people. They helped us put our lives back on track. I sent out thank you notes last week. Oh, I don't think I told you." Donnie paused to rustle some papers around.

"One of the thank you notes I wrote was to my old boss back there in Massachusetts. Do you remember Jason Doherty? I worked for him when he was starting out. I was his estimator and computer guy. He was doing great and he and I got along so well, then I had to move to Maryland and leave due to my health. Well anyway," Donnie continued, without waiting for his mother to answer his question. "He sent me a thousand dollar donation. I cried when I saw that. I haven't talked to him in years. So I sent him a thank you, and enclosed my email address and phone number. He wrote an email to me the other day saying that he has expanded his business and if I ever returned to

Mass, I had a job. I couldn't believe it. It got me to thinking Ma." Now he stopped talking, to see if she was listening. She was. "We moved out here so I could get a transplant. I did. I'm doing great. But we have no jobs, no friends to speak of, no family. Livvy and I want to move home, Ma. We miss the east coast. What do you think?"

"Wow Donnie. I think it's wonderful, but isn't it a little sudden? What do your doctors say? Where would you go, who would take care of you medically?" It was a bit of a shock. "You know I'd love you to be back here, Donnie. But you need to think this through carefully. You've been through a traumatic ordeal just a few months ago." As mother's do, Emma was worried about him trying to make a move across the country.

"Well of course we'll think it through and I'll talk to my doctors and see if they can refer me to a post transplant team back in Boston. We'll be careful and plan it out. Maybe you can help find us a place to live. I'll talk more to Jason to make sure he really means it about giving me a job. It won't be for a few months yet, I'm thinking maybe the end of March. Our lease is up on this apartment on April first."

Emma was blown away. They had talked about it. They were already making plans to move back home. As the shock wore off, excitement rushed in. Her baby was going to be able to come home. He was going back to work. He had another chance to live his life. Tears flooded her eyes and she sniffled, as she reached for a tissue.

"Are you crying again, Ma," Donnie laughed. "You are such a softy."

All of her children and grandchildren would be back together again. Family was so important. Emma couldn't wait to spread the news. But how would he manage getting his family, his car and all their furniture back across the country. Certainly he wasn't strong enough to manage all of that. A new worry for Emma. And it would be costly.

Emma notified her four clients that she would be moving slightly off the Cape however she could continue to do their bookkeeping. She had given up several other small clients in the past year when she flew out to be with Donnie. These four business owners were all on the cutting edge and she was able to do their record keeping and monthly financials via the internet and with a fax machine. It wasn't a great deal of income for her but it kept her busy and gave her a small cash flow when combined with the income she received from her father's estate. She would be fifty nine this year so she still needed to derive income to collect her social security when she turned sixty two. She thought once she got settled into her new house she just might pick up a few more clients as time went on, while Bill concentrated on his remodeling business. They were not rich by any means but they were comfortable and they both felt they would and could help their children as needed. Donnie's needs far exceeded those of her daughters and that made Emma feel a little guilty so she tried to make it up in other ways, like renting her house to Jessie for only five hundred dollars a month when she could easily get double that on the real estate market today. Katie being pregnant, she needed extra hands on help with little Ricky so Emma took him often to give Katie a break and Emma cooked meals for Katie's family. Emma was a great cook and enjoyed doing it. Katie hated to cook. And so did

Jess. Donnie was her only child that followed in her love of cooking.

She would be so happy to have him home again and cook together

again. She smiled with the memory of him helping her in Papa's

kitchen at the deli. They worked well side by side.

Chapter 23

Donnie had his third Bronc on December 18th, a week before

Christmas and the good news just filled him with thankfulness. He had

truly been blessed. The steroids had made his face puffy and his meds

disturbed his sleep, caused leg cramps and some dizzy spells and at

times his eyes didn't focus just right but other than those minor side

effects, Donnie was a walking miracle. His female surgeon said he was

the new poster child for a lung transplant. They were all amazed at his

fantastic progress. They told him they'd refer him to a good doctor

once he went back to Boston, but they were sorry to see him leave Los

Angeles. This Bronc was a good one, no infection and no more

rejection.

Christmas eve Emma and Bill had an Open House at their new

home and had invited friends and new neighbors as well as family to

drop by between the hours of four and seven p.m. Emma had cooked

up a storm and had lots of appetizers and nibbles along with Swedish

meatballs, crab stuffed mushrooms, devilled eggs and sandwiches in finger rolls. There was a non alcoholic punch as well as beverages of many varieties, beer and wine. Bill had Joe help him and they surrounded the house in tiny white lights. Emma covered the front door with a red tin foil paper and taped a big green ribbon to make it look like a wrapped gift. Bill had a spotlight on it, and that lighted the way for their guests on Christmas eve.

Some people came and went and others came and ate and drank and stayed. The kids played in the rec room downstairs and were well behaved as they were all dressed up in pretty new clothes.

Around seven thirty when all of the guests had gone and just the family remained they sat around the Christmas tree in the living room and opened their gifts. This was for the adults. The next day, Christmas, would be for the children. Early in the morning Emma and Bill would go over to Bill's old house, which now belonged to Lucy, Scott and Molly. They would watch Bill's granddaughter open her gifts and then they'd have a big breakfast. Later in the day, the newlyweds would go over to Katie's house where Jessie promised to help her mother cook a ham dinner and they would see what Ricky got from Santa Claus.

Charlie and Lenny invited Donnie and his family to Christmas Brunch at their place along with a few other close friends. At first, Donnie was inclined to turn down the invitation, having two active children but then Lenny mentioned that one of their friends was bringing their five year old and the kids would have fun, so Donnie accepted gratefully.

Charlie and Lenny had been such a huge help to Donnie, he could never thank them enough. Besides that, they had become close friends. When Donnie told them that they were going to move back east, Charlie was sad but Lenny piped up with a big smile and said "Hey, we have a new challenge…let's get Donnie home!" And they vowed to start work on how they could help Donnie move his family back to Massachusetts. Donnie told them that he would be forever in their debt and they both laughed and told him it was their pleasure. They were such happy people; it was so nice to be around them.

.

Chapter 24

Once the holidays were behind them, Bill and Emma got into a routine of normalcy. It was as if they had been married all their adult lives; they just fit together so well and complimented one another.

Emma spent her mornings on her computer after she cleaned up from breakfast. She worked a few hours doing bookkeeping for her clients and then she'd check on Facebook for any news from old friends. Today she decided to do some research with the help from their realtor friend, Mike, trying to find a suitable home for Donnie and his family. If he went back to work for Jason Doherty, he would have to be in a different part of the state, so before she got too far, she texted Donnie.

"Have you contacted Jason yet about a job? Will you need a home out by where you used to live? I'm going to start doing some research for you." She sent the text message at ten of five.

Two minutes later her cell phone rang. "Are you psychic Ma? I just got off the phone with Jason." Donnie laughed. He and his mother always had some special kind of connection but this was uncanny.

"I've been talking, texting and emailing him for a few weeks now. He just called to finalize the deal with me. Are you sitting down?" He teased her. He had some great news for her.

"He and a partner just purchased an apartment complex from a bank. It was in foreclosure. They got a great deal on it. But half of the apartments are empty and in need of repair. It's in Quincy near Wollaston Beach. His partner owns a single family home in Braintree at the Quincy line, on a side street, about fifteen minutes from the complex. It was his mother's house and it has been empty for the past four months since his mother died. He didn't know if he was going to sell it or keep it. He says we can have it to live in as part of the contract he wants me to sign as the Property Manager for the complex. He'll have work for Olivia too if she wants it…she can make her own hours and sometimes work from home. She will be cleaning apartments when someone moves out and doing some paper work stuff. He will pay her fifteen dollars an hour. I will get a monthly check plus a bonus for each unit I find a renter to occupy an empty apartment. So how is that for a deal? A home and a job for each of us, all in one." He was quite pleased with himself.

Emma was so happy for him. Her heart just swelled with joy.

"Okay smarty pants, you've got that all worked out, how are you doing planning your actual move?" She thought she would jab him a little, burst his big bubble. But he had a good come back.

"Don't be so smug. You forget. I have Charlie and Lenny working on that with me. They are fantastic Mom. They know so many people and they are so giving. I'm going to miss them when I'm gone. But don't you worry about it, we're working on it." He wasn't ready with final details to share with her just yet.

Emma put her phone back on the desk and scratched Mike's name off her list for things to do today. She wouldn't need his help to find Donnie a place to live. He was going to be just forty minutes up the highway from where she lived. Things were just falling into place, they must have been meant to be.

Emma's phone rang again. She smiled as she reached for it thinking it was Donnie with something to add.

"Ma." It was Katie. "My water broke half an hour ago and Joe isn't picking up his cell phone. Ricky is at pre-school. Can you come over and drive me to the hospital?"

"Oh good Lord, Katie, I'm half an hour away. What about Jessie?"

Katie began to sniffle. "She's at work, Mom. She just started her job last week. I can't ask her to leave her job."

"Katie. Listen to me. You need to get to the hospital. You can't wait at home for me. I'll meet you there. Call a neighbor or a taxi. Keep trying Joe. Where was he working today?"

"I don't know, Ma. We had a little tiff. He said he didn't feel well and didn't want to go to work today. I yelled at him. He had too many beers last night, no wonder he wasn't feeling well. I told the lazy ass to take an aspirin and go make some money to support his family. I was so mad at him. He slammed the door on his way out."

"Oh boy, Katie. Do you know if any of your neighbors are home?"

"I'll call a taxi if I can't find one. Mom, please meet me at the hospital. I don't want to do this alone. Please."

Emma's heart ached for her daughter. Her girls picked such losers to marry.

"I'll be there in half an hour honey. I'm leaving now."

Emma called Bill to give him the latest and to let him know that she didn't know when she'd be home. He said he'd call around and see if he could locate Katie's deadbeat husband.

Emma called Jessie at work using Bluetooth in her car. Jessie said she'd take an early lunch and go to get her sister if she wasn't already on her way. Emma thanked her.

A few minutes later Jessie called her back. She told her mother that Katie called the fire department around the corner from her house and they sent an EMT to transport her.

"She thinks fast under stress. She'll be there by the time I get there, Ma. Drive carefully. I'll take care of her. My boss told me it was okay if I needed the afternoon off, things were slow today anyway. He's a great guy, Ma. I love my new job"

While sitting in the waiting room Emma texted Donnie to tell him about Katie. Then she texted Bill to see if he located Katie's husband, Joe.

"Yes. He'll be there soon. The bartender is making him drink coffee and will provide him with a ride to the hospital. He was there when the bar opened." Bill didn't add what his feelings were about Joe. Emma had her own. Neither of them was good.

When Joe arrived, he was embarrassed to find his mother in law sitting in the waiting room. He asked where Katie was. He was supposed to be there when she had the baby. He sobered up fast when he found out she was at the hospital but he was still intoxicated and Emma wasn't about to allow him to go into the birthing room.

"Jessie is with her. She's her coach, and she's a nurse, so all is being taken care of Joe. Just sit there and wait for them to let you know. Do you want me to get you a cup of coffee?" Emma was trying very hard to keep her tongue civil.

"I'll go get it. I need to walk anyway. Do you want one, Emma?" Emma declined.

He helped himself from the pot that was in the waiting room. It was like mud but he needed a good strong cup of coffee. The coffee at the bar wasn't quite enough. He picked up a few cookies that was on the plate beside the machine. He sat down next to Emma. His head hung low as he nibbled his cookies and sipped his coffee.

"I'm sorry I wasn't around Emma. We had a little spat this morning. I guess I was feeling sorry for myself." Joe confessed to his mother in law. She just nodded. There was nothing for her to say. She didn't need to forgive. He needed to forgive himself first.

Jessie came out of the birthing room with a big smile. "Barbie Ann has arrived." She announced to her mother and Joe. Knowing it was going to be a girl, they chose the name on Christmas day when they were all sitting around the dinner table eating their ham dinner. "She weighs seven pounds and fourteen ounces."

Emma laughed right out loud. "Hey Ma, isn't that how much Donnie weighed? That's your special number, right?" Jess knew all about it, listening to them rant about it over the years.

"Oh yes. That's our number all right. How funny." Emma smiled. "when can we see them?"

Joe was already headed for the room where Jess had come from. No one was going to tell him to wait until the nurses cleaned up his baby daughter. He was the proud father. Pretty well sobered up too.

"Let's give them a few minutes alone," Emma suggested, knowing Joe probably was feeling like a heel at this point. She and Jessie each went for a fresh cup of coffee in the hospital cafeteria and carried it back to the room that held Emma's new grandchild.

Chapter 25

Barbie Ann was born at 1:47 in the afternoon, Emma's numbers, yet again. They followed her everywhere. She called Donnie after visiting briefly with her daughter and newest granddaughter.

"She is absolutely gorgeous. I think she's going to be a fair blonde unlike Ricky who takes after his dad with the dark hair and dark eyes. I think Barbie is going to take after my side of the family, either blonde or pale red. It's hard to tell but you can see how light her eyebrows are, that's a dead giveaway." Emma bored her son with all the little details that grandmother's notice in their kids' children.

"Donnie, please tell me, why do you and Katie name your children with nicknames instead of formal ones? This one is Barbie, not Barbara. Ricky is not Richard. You have Beth and Billy, not Elizabeth and William. What is it with you two? " Emma laughed, shaking her head, as she walked to her car in the hospital parking lot.

"We are just rebels, I guess Mom. Why do we need to be so conventional anyway?" He loved poking fun and teasing his mother.

"You christened me Donovan and yet you and everyone else

calls me Donnie. Why not cut out the formal name and go right for the name everyone will use? Makes sense to me and Katie I guess." It did make sense, sort of.

"Well, I can't wait until you move back home so you can see Katie's kids and your kids can get to grow up with their cousins. That will be so wonderful." Donnie agreed.

"Now we need Jessie to find a good man and give her some children before she gets too old," he said half kiddingly but feeling for his oldest sister who had no children.

"I'm not sure that she can have children, Donnie. She never came out and told me that but she recently had a miscarriage early in a pregnancy. Brad left when she told him that she was pregnant and then she lost it anyway.

"She had two miscarriages when she was married to Jack. I think that was the root of some of their problems. She wanted a house full of kids but both times when she got pregnant he was upset and said he didn't want any children. They fought about it. Then another time, she thought she was pregnant and she was so excited. She confided in me, but she was afraid to tell her husband. However it was a false alarm and she told me later that he told her he was glad she wasn't pregnant. He said he was going to get a vasectomy because he couldn't trust her using birth control. Their marriage didn't last much longer after that happened.

"It is so strange how people who can afford them and want children have such a hard time having them and others that probably shouldn't have kids, pop them out like candy." Donnie was a little too graphic for his mother's wishes but she understood.

Emma had been one of the fortunate ones who had no trouble at all getting pregnant. She had two girls in three years and two years later, she had Donnie.

"I hope Jess finds a nice guy this time. She hasn't done very well with her choices so far. But at least for now, she is through with school, and has found a nice job. She likes the doctor that she is working for; said he was a decent man. It figures, she'd take a job working for a pediatrician."

"I'm going over to Jessie's now, you know, to my old house.

She's going to pick up some Chinese food since we had no lunch, Bill has a meeting to attend anyway and they'll have dinner at the club when the meeting is over so this works out well for me. And we told Joe to come over and join us after he picks Ricky up at day care."

"That's cool, ma. I can't wait to get back there to be with family again."

Emma hadn't said those things to make him feel bad but apparently she didn't realize how lonely he had been living out on the west coast for the past few years.

Emma walked into her house, using her own key. Immediately she began picking up after Jessie. She had clothes dropped here and there and her bed was still unmade and her dirty-clothes hamper was over flowing even though there was a washer and dryer right in the hallway by the bathroom. Emma decided to throw a load of wash in for her daughter, shaking her head. She was never going to grow up enough to be a good housekeeper. While the white clothes sloshed around in detergent and bleach, Emma picked up the portable phone and put it back into its stand to recharge, and she straightened out some old newspapers and put the trash outside into the large receptacle. She wiped down the counter and the kitchen table and found the paper plates and grabbed some napkins and silverware just as Jessie pulled into the driveway. She carried a big bag full of cartons with a variety of Chinese appetizers, chicken chow mien and pork fried rice.

"I couldn't decide what I wanted. I was starving. So I got a little of everything," Jess said putting the shopping bag onto the table.

She kicked of her shoes and happened to hear the washing machine.

"Mom, you don't have to do my laundry, ya know. And thanks for tidying up." She shrugged her shoulders as if to say, that's just who I am. Sorry.

"Just trying to help my little girl. One day you will learn organization skills, maybe, or maybe not." Emma laughed. "Definitely NOT." Jessie laughed too in agreement with her mother.

Joe's pickup truck pulled into the driveway and Ricky came running into the house yelling "Nana. Nana." He ran into his grandmother's arms and she lifted him up in a big grandma hug.

"I've got a new baby sister," he announced. "Her name is BeeBee."

"I know you have a new baby sister. I saw her. Her name is Barbie."

"No Nana. I'm going to call her BeeBee. I like BeeBee better." They all laughed.

"Oh boy, here we go," said Joe, washing his hands at the kitchen sink. "GOD that smells so good. I can't tell you the last time we had Chinese. Katie can't stand the smell when she's pregnant."

They sat around the little dining room table filling their faces and talking at the same time. Jessie and Joe both had beer and Emma had diet soda. She had to drive home. Ricky drank water with his meals, something Katie taught him to do, just like she did.

When they had finished eating, Emma and Jessie cleaned up while Joe cleaned up his son who had sweet duck sauce all over his face and hands and his shirt. He took a twenty dollar bill out of his wallet and put it on the table, unsure who paid for the food, but wanting to make his contribution.

"That's not necessary, Joe. Take that money. You are going to need it with another mouth to feed." Jessie tried to hand the money back to her brother in law but his ego got in the way. He didn't want charity.

"Katie can feed the baby for the first few months anyway. Thanks for the grub. I've gotta get this little guy home." He picked up Ricky and let him kiss his Nana good bye, then a big hug and a kiss for Auntie Jess. "Thanks guys. It's been a long day. I'll get a baby sitter and go back up to see Katie a little later."

"I'll stop to see her on my way home. I'm going to leave here in a few minutes, but I won't be staying long." Emma told him so he didn't feel that he needed to rush back but he wouldn't have to share his wife with her mother when he was there either.

Emma walked down the hall and swapped Jess' laundry over to the dryer.

Do you want me to throw in another load of laundry Jessie?" She called out.

"No thanks Mom, I'll get to it tomorrow. Thanks anyway."

Famous last words, Emma was thinking with a sly grin on her face. At least her daughter would have clean undies for work the next day.

"Thanks for the Chinese food sweetheart. It hit the spot. Like Joe, I haven't had it for a long time. I forget how good it tastes when you don't eat it very often." Emma kissed her daughter good bye, thanking her for helping Katie deliver her baby girl.

Emma had a horrendous time trying to find a parking spot at the Cape Cod Hospital parking lot. It was prime time visiting hours. She got lucky as one car pulled out in front of her. She only stayed about twenty minutes with Katie, who was undoubtedly exhausted. As she exited the lobby to walk to her car, she saw Joe pulling in. She waved her arms in the air so he would follow her to grab her parking spot. He waved to thank her and she headed for home, over the bridge.

Chapter 26

Donnie had given his mother the address of the house he would be living in and asked her if she would go check it out and send him some pictures of the house and the neighborhood so on Saturday Emma and Bill took a ride to Braintree. She programmed her GPS with the address and off they went. Thirty five minutes later they were parked in front of the quaint two story older home. It was only minutes from the highway and in a nice quiet neighborhood on a dead end street.

Emma began taking pictures with her phone. The back yard was all fenced in with a chain link fence, enclosing the half acre treed lot. Out in back, off the kitchen was a nice sized deck with built in benches and a sturdy old picnic table. The table had a hole in the middle that probably once held an umbrella for shade.

They peeked in the sliding glass doors but couldn't see too much since the blinds had been pulled closed. Emma climbed up on the end of one of the benches and looked through the window that was over the sink. It was a good sized kitchen with all the appliances, seriously outdated, however. She wondered if they all still worked.

"Hello," the next door neighbor called from over the fence. "Can I help you with something?"

Emma and Bill walked over to the fence to introduce themselves and explain that they weren't merely trespassers but checking out the house their son was going to occupy.

"They will be moving here from California so he asked me to come and take some pictures of it and check out the neighborhood. They have two small children. Twins." Emma was trying to feel out this woman and see what she could learn about the neighbors. She got more than she bargained for. The woman invited them into her home and they had tea and some homemade biscuits she had just pulled out of the oven.

An hour later, as they were driving home, Emma sent five pictures to Donnie then called him.

"It's a charming old house, Donnie, needs some TLC but you can do that yourselves. The appliances could be updated, you might want to suggest to Jason. They look well worn. The house is about forty years old, has a new roof according to the next door neighbor. She is a lovely woman, lost her husband a few years ago. Her daughter moved in with her last year when she got divorced, she is a para-legal who takes the train into Boston every day. Her teenage granddaughter spends weekends with them. I guess she lives with her father during the week but we didn't get into that. Sally, that's the lady's name, said her granddaughter does a lot of babysitting, by the way."

Emma told him the back yard is lovely and private and fenced in. The elementary school is within walking distance. There's a McDonald's and an ice cream store practically within a stone's throw from that side street, on the main road. When she finished with all the details Donnie laughed.

"I sent you to check it out. I didn't think you would find out the forty year history on the place. You did well, Mom. Good Job." He snickered.

"We then took a ride over to the complex in Quincy where you will be working, just to clock the distance. Back roads took us fifteen minutes. We then hopped on the highway from there to go home and we passed the exit you'll use in five minutes, so I'd say the highway will be the quickest route for you to go. It's a big place, that complex, Donnie. Are you sure you can handle this position?"

"I'll do what I can, Ma. I have to try it. If I can't, we'll cross that bridge when I get there. Please don't worry. I love you, Ma."

"Worrying about my kids is what I do best, Donnie." Emma smiled. Out of the corner of her eye, she saw Bill nodding his head in agreement. She reached out to smack his arm and he winked at her.

The following day, Emma and Bill took another ride and went down to the Cape to visit Katie. Emma had cooked some casseroles to bring them, along with a bag full of groceries. Bill was looking forward to meeting Barbie for the first time. For a big tough guy, he was so kind and gentle and he loved little kids.

Joe had been on his best behavior since the baby was born. Knowing Emma and Bill were coming to visit, he scrubbed the kitchen floor and vacuumed for Katie. He adored his new baby girl but he was so attentive to Ricky so his little nose wouldn't get bent out of shape.

Joe took Ricky with him everywhere he went, since he didn't have to work for a few weeks. He had planned to take some time off when the baby was born. Katie teased him that he'd probably get her pregnant again right away so he could take more time off work, but she was glad to have his help.

Emma brought fresh hoagie rolls from the bakery and lots of cold cuts and cheeses, potato chips, pickles and ice cream for dessert. Ricky asked if they were going on a picnic.

"Well Ricky, we can have our picnic right here at home. Let's get a blanket and we'll spread it out on the living room floor and we'll all sit around and eat. How's that sound honey?" Nana was making a game out of having lunch.

"Nana it sounds like fun but I don't think Mommy can get down on the floor. She is getting old, ya know. She walks real slow now that she had BeeBee."

Emma held back her laugh. "I guess you are right, Ricky. Mommy IS getting old. And aren't you smart to notice that? You are getting so grown up." And she glanced at Katie who also was trying not to laugh out loud at her son. Emma faced Katie so Ricky would not hear her. "Out of the mouth of babes."

Emma glanced around the room. "Where did Bill go?" she asked Katie.

"He's in the baby's room. He wanted to hold her, why?"

Together they walked into the nursery and there was Papa Bill sitting in the rocking chair with the baby cuddled in his arms. He was in seventh heaven. Emma snapped a quick picture with her iPhone.

"That's a great picture, Billy. You are such a great grandpa." Emma loved her husband. How lucky she was to have been given a second chance with him in her life.

"I think she's the prettiest baby I've ever seen," he said very softly, looking into the baby's adorable face. "I think she's going to be a red headed devil," he teased.

The hours passed quickly and Emma could see her daughter was fading, so she said her farewell and she and Bill headed back to Manomet. They were talking about the baby on their way home.

"She sure is a cutie pie, so delicate and fair." Bill commented.

"I noticed she took deep breaths. I could almost count her little ribs. I guess I just forgot how small they start out. I was almost afraid I'd break her in half." He chuckled.

"Yeah, she is really fair skinned and even her hair and eyebrows are light. I think it makes her look smaller. Donnie weighed the same but he was darker complected. I just don't remember him looking that small. But she'll grow fast, you just wait and see."

"I can just see it now, I know it in my bones, she's going to be a hellion." Bill was teasing his wife. "You redheads are all devils."

They stopped at a local pizza place on their way home and each had a glass of wine and a slice of cheese pizza.

Chapter 27

The weeks were flying by. St. Patrick's Day was quickly approaching. Emma and Bill decided to have a big family shindig and cook a corned beef and cabbage dinner and invite some friends over as well. Since St. Patty's day fell on Tuesday this year, the couple thought they would have their party on the preceding Sunday, when people didn't have to work. Emma told them to come any time after noon and dinner would be around 2 pm. Bill had borrowed a CD from a fellow fireman that had all the Irish music on it. He went with Emma to the party supply store to buy some decorations and paper products. Then he helped Emma decorate the house in green balloons and streamers. It looked festive.

She bought three large corned beefs and cooked them up the day before, reserving the broth she cooked them in with the pickling spices. The roasts shrunk when cooked and she wanted to make sure to have enough. It was the red beef so it would be great for sandwiches the next day if there was any left over.

That day she had Bill slice it up and she put it into a deep aluminum pan, with some of the broth, covered it with tin foil and warmed it up in the oven. She cooked the red bliss potatoes, onions and cabbage in the rest of the broth, adding a little more water as needed. She cooked the carrots and beets separately. She remembered what her father taught her and how to prepare the meal from the old deli days. They set up a long table in the rec room downstairs where the music was being played. She and Bill would plate the meal and then they could carry it downstairs to eat dinner. There was Irish soda bread all sliced on the table. She had green food coloring to put into the beer for effect.

Their neighbors from across the street, Tim and Sally Walker arrived a little after one o'clock with several bottles of wine, both red and white, and a bouquet of green carnations. Another couple came. She made cup cakes with green frosting and little plastic shamrocks on them.

Katie had her two kids all dressed in green, and she wore a long kelly green sweater with black tights. She had already lost all of her baby weight and was looking good, but very tired still. Joe wore his leprechaun hat and green suspenders with his jeans.

Jessie was a little more reserved since she had her new boyfriend with her to meet the family for the first time. She was dating her boss, the doctor. She wore an off white dress with three quarter sleeves and a hand crocheted deep green sweater vest. She had a green velvet ribbon in her hair and she looked very pretty, Emma thought, shaking hands with Dr. Drake. He was not much taller than Jessie but quite good looking with dark hair and dark eyes. He wore a pale green button down collar dress shirt with khakis.

Emma was happy that her children made the effort to dress for the festivities. After all, her grandparents had come from Tipperary and her father, Francis Patrick McNally loved this holiday. It was always a great time at the deli on St. Patrick's day, March 17th. He was with her in thought today.

They did FaceTime with Donnie and his family once everyone was gathered around, just before they sat down to dinner.

"Wish you were here, honey," Emma said to him.

"We'll be there next year, Ma. So you can start planning your next year's party."

He told her that Charlie and Lenny once again had pulled a rabbit out of a hat for them and they had all their plans set. They were beginning to pack up their belongings to move back east. He said he'd fill her in later in the week when they had made all the final arrangements. "Have a good time today, and don't eat too much." He snickered. "Oh and tell Bill not to worry if Charlie doesn't answer his cell. He and Lenny are sponsoring a sing-along down at a bar they go to, and they're feeding the homeless. It will probably be busy and very noisy."

Charlie and Lenny were always doing something for other people. For Donnie they were making a another sacrifice, one last time. They were going to take vacation time and they would drive a U-Haul truck with Donnie's furniture and tow his SUV back home to Massachusetts. They planned on spending a few days there visiting family and old friends and then they'd fly back to California. They wouldn't take a dime. They had passed the hat around and collected funds to pay for the gas and their expenses, along with airfare for

Donnie and his family and since the guys were always doing for other people, their friends stepped up to the plate and donated generously to support this move.

Donnie called his mother on the actual St. Patrick's day and greeted her like he did every March 17th. "Happy St. Papa's Day". He remembered how much his grandfather enjoyed that day and now that he was in heaven, Donnie considered him to be a saint. Emma got a big kick out of it.

Donnie asked her what she was doing on Tuesday, the 31st of March. She said she had no idea, why?

"That's the day we are coming home and we'll need a ride from Logan airport. Do you think you can pick us up?" He knew what her response would be, but he had checked with Bill before he made that actual plane reservations. Just to make sure.

Emma beamed. The day was finally approaching. Her baby was coming home.

"Charlie and Lenny are going to drive a truck with our stuff and tow my car. They are leaving on Sunday the 28th. We'll load the truck the day before on Saturday. It will be all ready. They said they'd' probably get up around four in the morning to get going before the heavy traffic clogged the highways."

"Well, where will you go? What will you sleep on?? Emma the worrier kicked in.

"We will spend most of the day cleaning up around here then we'll go over to Charlie's place to sleep that night and Monday. A shuttle will pick us up early Tuesday and take us to the airport. We will arrive in Boston around three thirty. Can't wait to get home, Ma. I'm so tired of being here."

Emma could tell he'd been pushing to get all of these plans taken care of.

"I have another request for you. Can you go to Quincy and get the keys for the house we're renting and then go to the house? Jason said he'll have a cleaning crew go all through it and clean it up and check everything this week, but I just want you to double check and see what we'll need. We'll go right from Logan to the house, if that's okay with you guys."

"Yes my dear boy, Momma will take care of that for you. Give me Jason's number so I can call him to make arrangements to get the keys. Great idea, Donnie. But Donnie, your furniture won't be at the house. Lenny and Charlie can't get there in a few days, can they?"

"Good thinking Ma. I knew I called you for a reason. I know they were planning on taking turns driving, but they might not make it that fast. We'll have to have a Plan B."

Emma took a ride to Quincy on Friday and met with Jason and thanked him for offering her son both a job and a place to live. They had coffee and talked for over an hour. Emma had met Jason several times when Donnie worked for him in the past. He had grown his business and it was flourishing. He liked Donnie and was glad he could help him out.

"He was a good worker, but more than that, Emma, he is a good person. Everyone liked working with Donnie. Now, if you find something that isn't working or needs replacing, just give me a call." He offered her one of his cards. She thanked him again and left to go checkout the house where the painting crew was just finishing up.

When Emma walked in the front door, that had been left open to air out from the smell of freshly painted walls, she was surprised to see all the appliances in the kitchen had been replaced with brand new ones, the stove, microwave, refrigerator and dishwasher were all stainless steel and sparkling. She was more than pleased that Jason and his partner took the liberty to do that for her son.

The old yellowed wallpaper had been removed and every room had a fresh coat of paint. The few rooms that had carpet had been shampooed and the hard wood floors had been sanded and refinished. It looked like a new house. Some of the old worn boards out on the deck had been replaced or repaired. The house showed well. Olivia would be happy here and if the wife is happy, the husband is happy. She couldn't wait to see them walk around in their new home, it was so much bigger than the townhouse that they had been living in. It had a master bedroom with its own bathroom on the first floor along with a nice workable kitchen and separate dining room and living room with a fireplace. Donnie would love that. A half bath was in the hallway.

Upstairs there were two huge bedrooms with big long closets and another full bathroom. She checked the faucets and made sure the water was turned on. She went back to the first floor and decided to check out the basement, where she found a brand new washer and dryer and a soap sink had been installed and a clothes line was strung from one pole to another. How thoughtful. She wondered if a woman had been part of the cleaning crew to suggest that. The kids would be very pleased moving in here. She would tell Donnie to call in a lock smith to change all the locks however, once he arrives. You can't be sure who has keys floating around out there. He could always give a copy of the new keys to Jason when he did it. She made herself a mental note.

On Sunday, Bill went with Emma to the garden center at Home Depot and they bought some large planters for the outside of Donnie's new house and then they bought some potting soil and fertilizer. They knew Olivia loved to garden and that was one thing she had to give up living in California in an apartment complex surrounded by cement walkways and a parking garage. It was a little early to plant flowers

just yet, but it was their welcome home gift to Olivia. They went to the

house and placed them at the entrance on either side of the front stairs.

The planters were a bright blue ceramic, giving some color to the

natural weathered shingled house. There was a small mud room

enclosed as you entered so they put the potting soil there for later use.

Emma showed Bill around and he was impressed. The place

was very presentable. As a man who did renovations and repairs, he

checked things out more closely than Emma had done on Friday. He

spent half an hour down in the basement and found an old wooden

ladder to get up onto the roof. Even the gutters had been cleaned and

oiled.

"Everything looks good to me. I'm not sure about that chimney

but it looks okay. Maybe Donnie can ask Jason to find out the last time

it was used, or get a chimney sweep in to make sure it hasn't got a

buildup of creosote. Other than that, it's ready to move in."

Emma was so happy that Bill took the time to do a thorough

inspection. Olivia was a good housekeeper, and since Donnie needed things as germ free as possible, she knew they would take good care of this house, even with two little rug rats running around. Maybe they could even get a dog with a fenced in back yard, it wouldn't be too much trouble, but she'd let them get settled before suggesting that.

On their way back home, Emma texted Donnie and told him that she and Bill had done a full scale inspection and the house was all set and ready to go. He was thrilled to know that Bill had taken the interest to do that for them.

"Olivia will sleep better now. I think she was a little worried about moving into a house sight unseen, but if you guys both say it's good, I know it IS good." There was happiness in his words. Excitement. He was looking forward to beginning the next phase of his life. And doing it near his family.

Chapter 28

It had been a cold and snowy winter for New England, especially in the Boston area however, March had been a mild month and the snow was gradually melting. Some days the temperature was into the fifties and for Boston, it felt wonderful. Spring had really arrived.

On March 30th, the temperatures dropped as the day went on and by mid afternoon the snow began to fall once again. Everyone was so darn tired of the snow and ice, they just did not want to deal with more snow, yet the forecast was for another Nor'easter with possibly another foot of snow to contend with.

Emma was so concerned. Donnie, Olivia and their two children were supposed to fly from California the next day, once the snow had mounted. She worried their plane would be cancelled, would they be forced to sleep in the LAX airport, waiting for a cancelled flight to be rescheduled? They would spend two nights at Charlie's, and take a shuttle to the airport, after locking up the condo. They told Charlie that they'd leave the spare key locked inside but when they heard about the weather forecast Donnie called Charlie on his cell.

Charlie was riding as a passenger while Lenny was driving the rental truck. They had been driving since four o'clock on Sunday morning, only stopping for fuel and eats. They were getting ready to stop for dinner and change drivers when Charlie answered Donnie's call.

"Not sure you guys have heard the weather but Boston is having a Nor'easter. The snow began a few hours ago. I'm not sure our plane will take off tomorrow. I just wanted you to know, we may be spending an extra day here in sunny California." Donnie was not happy about spending any more time there than they absolutely had to. He wanted to go home and begin his new life.

During the night the snow kept mounting and the wind kept blowing causing three foot snow drifts. At seven in the morning Logan Airport was shut down and the snow still fell. Donnie called ahead before leaving for the airport and was told it was not yet cancelled only delayed by two hours. He then called the shuttle service to reschedule a later pick up.

Olivia was so happy they had booked a direct flight and didn't have to change planes and get stuck somewhere half way across the country. Leaving a few hours later was fine. The kids could stay in the apartment and watch television. Olivia kept herself busy cleaning up and making sure the condo would be left in the impeccable shape it was in when they arrived.

She then prepared some sandwiches and snacks to take with them on the plane. Donnie was texting with friends and family, trying to keep himself occupied. When he began to pace back and forth, Olivia told him to go outside and get some warm fresh air because it would be cold and wet when they arrived in Boston. He went aggreeingly.

He walked around the block, taking deep fresh breaths. He thought by the time they arrived in Massachusetts it would be spring. He had forgotten that they still got freak snowstorms the end of March and even into April. He remembered wearing boots, hat and mittens over his Easter suit to church one year as a teenager. But he smiled, in spite of the weather; he'd be back home surrounded by his family. He couldn't wait.

The shuttle van arrived exactly at noon and they all piled in along with the other two people going to the airport. Traffic was a bear, stop and go. Donnie was getting tense and Olivia sensed his anxiety. They were the last ones to be dropped off and he and Olivia each grabbed a suitcase after putting back packs on the kids. The line for the security check was incredibly long but they had checked in online and were allowed to go through the pre-boarding line without having to remove shoes and belts. It saved them so much time.

Then they had to get to the gate. They walked slowly with the kids in tow, pulling their suitcases behind them. Donnie never could have done this prior to his surgery. The gate was almost down at the end.

"Daddy can we get a big pretzel?" Beth asked, eyeing one in a kiosk along the way.

"Not just yet, baby girl. Let's go check in first and see how much time we have, okay sweetheart? If we have time, Daddy will come back and buy you and Billy pretzels". Even with new lungs, his speech sounded winded to Olivia. He was only six months out from his transplant. That wasn't a lot of time.

Their flight was due to leave around two p.m. Originally it was supposed to take off just before noon and arrive in Boston at 8:22 with the time change. Now they would be getting in around ten thirty.

"DELAYED" the sign read at their gate. New time of departure scheduled for Three fifteen.

"Oh God" Olivia said with a big sigh. She was stressed to the max.

"Daddy, now can we go get our pretzels, please?" Beth was jumping up and down on her tippy toes, pleadingly.

Donnie smiled. "Sure baby girl, we have plenty of time now for pretzels." He looked at his wife. "Do you want one Liv?"

"Sure why not? A pretzel sounds good about now." Olivia said she'd stay with the luggage and the 4 seats they managed to find side by side. Donnie took his children's hands and walked back to the kiosk where they sold large, warm pretzels and drinks.

As they sat there munching on their treats, Olivia turned to Donnie who was staring out into space.

"I feel so bad that your mother has to come pick us up. Do you think we should take a shuttle or taxi instead? It will be so late by the time we get there."

"I don't know what shuttles run at midnight, Liv and we can't afford taxi cab fares from Boston to Braintree. Besides, Mom has the keys to the house. She'll be fine. She wants to see us anyway." Donnie smiled. "I'll text her and let her know we're being delayed again and see how the weather is now."

After getting his mother's reply, he told his wife that the snow had stopped and they were opening some runways slowly. "Mom said not to worry about the time, she and Bill will be there no matter what time we get in."

"You've got the best mother, Donnie. I love her." Olivia really did love her mother in law and not every wife can say that.

At three ten they began boarding people travelling with children.

Chapter 29

In the meantime, it had been a terrible storm and Cape Cod got hit hard.

"Mom, just wanted you to know, the whole street is without power. Clayton is on his way over here to pick me up so I'll be spending the night at his place, if he can make it." Emma received Jessie's text message about five o'clock. She read it aloud to Bill.

Clayton Drake was her employer, the pediatrician she worked for, who had become romantically involved with Jessica. He made Jess feel so special that her whole outlook on life had improved and she was changing and growing and Emma was so very pleased that for the first time in her life, her daughter had finally found real love. Clay doted on Jess, bought her gifts, took her to nice places, even took her clothes shopping and paid for everything.

Emma texted her back. "Be careful and keep me posted. I love you."

Emma then put in a call to Katie who also lived on the cape. Emma was surprised that she hadn't heard from her all day. And when

Katie answered the phone, Emma knew something was wrong.

"Hey Katie. Are you okay honey? I just wanted to check on you and the kids. Jess lost her power at the cottage." Emma was trying to feel Katie out.

"I haven't had power in over two hours, Ma. The baby is crying and hungry. Joe went to the store over an hour ago and hasn't returned, and he isn't answering his cell. I just hope he's not in some bar drinking. And then I get mad for thinking that since he's been so good since the baby was born. What if something happened to him?" Katie sniffed as she wiped tears from her eyes.

Emma could hear the baby crying.

"Have you got candles and a flashlight, honey? Is there anything I can do for you?"

"I'm okay Mom. I've got a flashlight and a few candles. I've got a gas stove so I'll be okay. I just wish Joe would come home to be with me. Thanks anyway. Ma, I gotta go feed this kid. She is the hungriest baby, all she wants to do is eat and sleep," she chuckled a little bit as she bounced the baby in her arms.

"Donnie's plane is due to come in about midnight so we have to go pick them up." Emma wanted to give details but Katie was too preoccupied with her own situation.

"Good luck Ma. I'm surprised that he is still coming in this weather."

Katie said again that she had to go so Emma hung up the phone and talked to Bill. She didn't know what she could do if she drove down to Katie's but she couldn't chance it in the snow and ice and still make it into Boston for Donnie.

"She'll be okay. Maybe Joe got stuck in a snow bank. She told you not to worry." Bill tried to calm her fears, knowing it was probably a waste of his time. Emma worried. That's just what Emma did.

Bill went outside to use his snow blower once again to clear a path from the house to the driveway and then he cleared the mound of snow the plow placed at the edge of his driveway. He was glad they didn't have far to go to get to the highway. The radio said it was clear and had been sanded.

Two hours later Jessie called her mother from her cell.

"Ma, don't freak out, okay. I'm at the hospital. It's okay. We found Joe. He slipped off the road, hit a patch of ice, and he crashed into a tree. If Clay hadn't come to get me, we never would have found him. He was probably there maybe an hour before we found him. I just happened to call Katie while I waited for Clay and she told me Joe had gone to Shaw's Supermarket for a few things she forgot to pick up. So I had Clay drive that back road from the market to Katie's house. No one was out, Ma. He would've been there til daylight. We called 9-1-1 and they rushed him here. I told Katie I'd come and check him out…they're treating him now and he'll be released so Clay and I will drive him home. Just didn't want you to worry."

"You should have seen Clay when we found Joe, slumped over, head bleeding. He just sprung into action. Oh Ma, he is so special. I love this guy, Ma." Jessie was beaming and Emma could tell.

"Oh yeah, and Katie told me to tell you, they got their lights back on."

Emma breathed a sigh of relief. She was so happy that her two girls stayed so close to one another. She was blessed with wonderful children.

She heard Bill stomping his feet to pound the snow off of his boots. She heard his voice and realized he was talking on his cell phone. She went to the door by the garage and let him in, helping him remove his wet gloves and his jacket. He kissed her forehead and slipped his feet out of his boots by the back door. Emma had placed a boot tray there for them when they would come and go. In his stocking feet he walked over to the kitchen counter and sat down, all the time talking to Charlie and laughing about their freak snow storm the last day of March.

"Charlie and Lenny just finished eating at a truck stop and they decided they'd drive a few more hours then put up for the night. They were both pretty beat up so figured five or six hours of sleep and a hot shower would be good. They're making good progress. He told me to get rid of this stuff, although he used another word to describe the snow. He said when he gets here he wants to see green grass and blooming flowers. I told him to take his time." Bill laughed out loud.

"We have a few hours before we need to leave to go to the airport, Bill. Why don't you go lie down for a little rest? I'll watch some television and check with the airport." Emma was too wired to even consider a short nap for herself. Between worrying about her daughters and Donnie's flight, she was ready to run a marathon with the adrenaline flowing.

"Good idea, hon. Thanks. Wake me at ten thirty. We'll leave about eleven fifteen."

Chapter 30

After several conversations with her son, Emma talked Donnie
into staying with her and Bill in Manomet until their own furniture
arrived with Charlie and Lenny. Especially now with the snow. The
house was on a side street which had not been plowed since noon time.
They had no place to sleep or sit or eat or television for the kids. It
only made sense. She had to pound it into her son's thick head. When
he first thought of going right to the house from the airport, he thought
his furniture would already be there for one thing. And he was
thinking there was no snow on the ground for another. He had been
able to get the water and electricity turned on and switched into his
name but the house was cold and damp and not a place where he
should be staying with this horrible weather. So he conceded.

Emma said they'd bring the snow blower over and let them see
the place the next day, but they would stay with them until the house
was ready. Donnie finally gave in. So Emma checked the downstairs
rec room where she had set up two blow up mattresses for her
grandchildren to sleep on. There were blankets and pillows and games

to play and the big TV. The kids would be fine down there. And Donnie and Olivia would sleep upstairs in the guest bedroom and have their own bathroom. Everything was clean and ready.

At ten thirty she woke Bill who was softly snoring, sound asleep. At first he didn't know where he was. While he slept, she whipped together a quiche Lorraine and made tea for them to have before venturing out in the cold.

They had no trouble getting into Logan. The highway was nicely plowed and there were no cars on the road other than big trucks sanding.

Donnie's plane was due to land at twelve oh five. It was April first, Fool's Day.

There were people sleeping on their luggage on the floor and in chairs, waiting for a rescheduled flight to get them out of Boston. But other than that, the place was eerie. All concessions were closed. There were no airline workers manning the counters. Just a few workers at the security check point. Bill tried to get access to meet Donnie's family at the gate but they would not allow them to go through security without a boarding pass.

So they found a place to sit by the windows but there was nothing to see in the blackness. They watched the screens for arrivals and Donnie's flight said 'on time'. Yeah, on time after three delays.

Bill sat and rested his eyes. It was midnight. Five more minutes. Emma was restless so she walked around. You could hear the heels of her boots on the tiled floor. It was the only sound around them.

"Emma, please, come sit down," Bill requested. Her pacing was driving him crazy. She smiled and sat back down and reached over to hold his hand.

All of a sudden there was pandemonium. People began running, others ran to the windows and you could hear sirens off in the near distance. Emma went to the windows and saw colored lights.

"What happened?" she asked the man standing next to her.

"I heard someone say a plane slid on the ice and went off the runway." He replied.

"Oh my God." Emma's hands covered her mouth and her heart

began to pound in her chest.

Before long all the sleeping people were milling around trying to find out what happened…someone had an app on his iPad that connected to the airport and they showed a plane that had skidded when it landed and the nose was almost into the icy water off the side of the runway. There were fire engines and ambulances and police cruisers all around it. They had opened the doors and the passengers were sliding down the inflatable slides and climbing down the stairs that were pushed over to the plane. People were screaming and crying.

Bill appeared beside his wife and put his arm around her shoulders.

"We don't know if that is Donnie's plane, Emma. Hold it together." He was trying to comfort her.

People were yelling and asking each other where the plane came from. It was only about five minutes but seemed like an eternity to Emma when they learned that the plane had come from Chicago's O'Hare airport.

Emma nearly collapsed into Bill's arms, she was so relieved. She burst into tears, unable to contain them any longer. He led her back to their seats and tried to get her to relax.

"You don't want Donnie to see you fall apart like this. It was not his plane. He is due here any minute. Pull yourself together. You need to be happy to see him and Olivia and the kids. Let them see that beautiful smile." He pulled her into a tight hug and rocked her for a minute.

Twenty five grueling minutes later, Donnie and his family came walking through the doors from the secured part of the airport, lugging their suitcases behind them. Emma and Bill hurried over to meet them and hug and kiss them.

"They had us circling the airport for almost fifteen minutes. They said they had to clear the runway, but there are all kinds of fire engines and stuff out there. What happened?" Donnie was curious.

Bill grabbed the carry on suitcase from Olivia and they began to walk towards the parking garage. "We'll tell you all about when we get to the car."

Chapter 31

The next day Donnie's children just wanted to go out and play in the snow. They hadn't seen snow since they were practically babies. But of course, they had no snow boots or mittens so Nana to the rescue. She put sox on their hands and covered their shoes in plastic bags held up with elastics. It was still very cold so Emma knew they wouldn't be outside for very long. She dressed up warm too and went out to show them how to build a snowman.

It was a brilliant sunny morning with blue skies and no wind. It was supposed to hit forty degrees by afternoon.

Donnie was standing at the front picture window watching his kids with his mother make snow angels and he smiled, listening to them laugh and giggle. Olivia was in the kitchen making hot chocolate and oatmeal for breakfast.

The kids and Nana came in through the garage and they stomped their feet to shake the snow off them. Emma had them throw their plastic bag-boots right into the big trash can in the garage and they put their sock-mittens on the shelf out there to dry. She hung their jackets and hats on the coat rack Bill built right outside the kitchen door.

Their noses and cheeks were pink and they were so excited and happy.

"Run downstairs now and put on some nice dry clothes," Olivia instructed. "I laid them out for you." She turned to Emma. "Thank you for playing with them Nana. That was a real special treat for them."

The kids ran downstairs, laughing and talking and anxious to change into nice warm dry clothes so they could have some cocoa and oatmeal with raisins.

The children sat down at the little table and chair set that Emma had picked up at a thrift store the prior week, knowing when the children would be arriving. She had a special place for it set up by the bay window that overlooked the back yard. The four adults sat at the regular kitchen table and had coffee and fresh cinnamon buns that Olivia pulled from the oven minutes before, along with the quiche she had made the night before. After breakfast, Bill and Emma would take the family to Braintree to see the house where they would be living after they stopped at the Hanover Mall to buy snowsuits, boots and mittens for the children.

When they arrived at the new house, the kids ran through the empty house, laughing and yelling to one another. They each chose which room they wanted for their own bedrooms. Olivia just kept smiling as Emma pointed out all the features in the house. Bill walked around with Donnie doing his own presentation.

"Can we go out, Mommy? I want to build a snowman in the back yard." Billy told Olivia.

"Sure. Let's put on your new boots and snowsuits first though, Okay? I need to run out to the car to get them."

Emma took a walk out back to make sure everything was safe for the children, then she went back inside to help Olivia dress the children.

Bill unloaded the snow blower from the back of his SUV and Emma grabbed the shovel. Donnie approached them saying he could shovel the walk and took the shovel away from his mother.

"It's okay Mom. I'll take my time and go easy. I'll call you if I need you to take over. Go out back and play with the kids." His smile was so warm and appreciative.

Emma relieved Olivia so she could go help her husband shovel the walk and clean off the front porch with a broom. When the work was done, they went out back to see what the kids were doing and Donnie reached for his phone. He took a picture of the snowman that Nana and the children had made, complete with dark colored rocks for the eyes and mouth. He texted the picture to Charlie saying "wish you were here".

Charlie wrote back saying "where are all the blooming flowers?" Bill laughed.

Then his phone rang. "Hey Charlie, where are you guys now? We just finished shoveling, could've used your help."

"With luck we should arrive sometime late tomorrow night. Text me the address so I can plug it into the GPS. Are we going to Donnie's place or yours, dad?"

"Well, if you get here late at night, you might as well take a motel room then we'll meet you over at Donnie's the next morning. If you get here in daylight, you should go to Donnie's. I'll send you his address. There are several motels right off the highway in Quincy and Braintree. If you want, I can make a reservation for you but I doubt that it will be necessary."

So the plan was in motion. They'd put up at a motel, get a good night's rest and a hot shower then Saturday they'd drive the truck over to Donnie's new place and begin unloading. Donnie and his family would spend the first night in their new house and Charlie and Lenny would spend some time at Bill and Emma's place.

On the way back to Manomet they stopped to pick up submarine sandwiches for lunch. They had built up a roaring hunger being outside in the snow. After lunch, Bill took Donnie and Olivia to go look at cars. Now that Donnie was well enough to drive again, they would need a second vehicle so Donnie could go to work each day. It was a whole new ballgame. Emma stayed home to watch the children while they took a nap. She sat down with a book she had been reading and with everyone gone and the house being so quiet, Nana fell fast asleep in Bill's recliner with her feet up.

She was awakened by a clap of thunder and the down pour of heavy rain. The house was dark. The kids must have heard the thunder as well because they were pounding up the stairs in search of a grown up. They were frightened.

"Nana. What was that noise?" Beth was hugging her grandmother's legs.

"It is just thunder, honey. Didn't you ever have rain in California?"

"Not like that." She said.

"Where is Mommy and Daddy?" Billy asked, while clinging to his Buddy, the stuffed dog. Then he added, "I'm hungry Nana. Can I have a cookie?" Emma took them into the kitchen and turned on the lights.

The children were sitting at their special little table eating chocolate chip cookies and drinking milk when their parents came home.

"Success." Said Bill as he greeted his wife with a peck on the cheek. "These kids know what they want when they see it. We'll pick it up tomorrow afternoon. Once that rain started, the salesman conceded and accepted their offer. He just wanted to close up shop and go home." Bill laughed. Bill grabbed a cookie and went into the other room.

"So what did you buy, Donnie?" Emma asked as she handed a bag of cookies out for her son to take a few.

"Liv liked the little yellow Volkswagen bug but it was too small. We agreed on the Honda Civic. Its only three years old, practically like new. It will be a good car for me to go back and forth in." Donnie reached for a glass to pour himself some milk to wash the cookies down.

The phone rang. It was Katie. "Hey you guys, what are you doing? Is it raining there? Its pouring here. I was going to take the kids up to see Donnie and the kids but I don't want to drive in this weather. Everything will be flooded, for God's sake. One day it snows, then we get rain. Good ole New England; if you don't like the weather, wait a minute. It'll change." Katie said sarcastically. She was not happy.

"Where is Joe, Katie? Is he working?" Emma asked her daughter.

"Well he went to work this morning. No telling where he is now. He started drinking again about a week ago. He's probably at his favorite watering hole." Katie sounded disgusted but Emma knew enough not to pry. If Katie wanted to tell her more, she would.

"We were just having milk and cookies. Bill took Donnie and Liv out to buy a new car so he can go back and forth to work."

"Hey mom, have you talked to Jess lately? She is really hooked on this guy, ya know. I mean heavy duty in love. They are together all the time." Katie was giving her mother a heads up because she knew it wouldn't be long before Jess moved out of Emma's cottage to live with Dr.Clay. Emma appreciated hearing it since she had not spoken to Jessie since the snow storm.

Thinking of the storm Emma connected the dots with what Katie said a few minutes ago.

"Katie, the night Joe had his accident, had he been drinking?

You said he started drinking over a week ago, right? I don't mean to pry honey, just curious if that's why he had the accident. I know it was icy, but you seemed very upset that night."

"You don't miss a trick, do ya, Mother?" Emma hated it when her daughter called her "Mother" but she held her tongue. "He went out that night to buy beer. He had stopped and, according to what he told me, he only had ONE beer at the bar before leaving to go to the store. He said the snow was coming down pretty hard so the bartender was closing early. So he was not drunk when he had the accident, if that's what you are asking."

Katie was defending her husband and that was okay with Emma. Normally she was the one complaining about him. Emma just hoped she didn't have her blinders on. She didn't want Katie to get hurt. But she didn't want her to be in denial either. Joe had a drinking problem and it was apparent that he couldn't manage it by himself.

Emma needed to change the subject. "Charlie and Lenny should be here tomorrow night and we're all going over to Donnie's new place on Saturday to unload and help them unpack, if you are interested. Bring the kids; we'll all help each other. Tell Jess."

Katie said she would definitely be there and would call for details later. She told her mother that Joe just walked in the door and her voice sounded a little more calm.

Friday night about eight o'clock Bill's cell phone rang while he was watching a little television in the 'rec' room with Donnie and the grandchildren. Emma was upstairs helping Olivia pack up things to move to their new house the next day. They planned to leave right after breakfast, nice and early.

"Hello," Bill said into his phone, walking away from the noisy television.

"Hey dad, just wanted to let you know that we made it. We found some cheap motel off the highway. I think we're in Quincy. GPS says we only have ten miles to go to get to Donnie's house from here, so that's cool." Charlie sounded very tired.

"Lenny is inside, checking in. I've been driving. It is better if just one of us checks in. Out in California two guys checking into a motel is no big deal. Out here in Puritan country, not so cool. So just one of us checks in and gets a room with two beds and everyone is happy." He joked about his sexual preference but it was a serious issue at times with some people. Bill totally understood. He felt a little strange at first when he went out to visit them, not knowing that they slept in separate rooms. But he was totally fine with the living arrangement they had. Their condo had 2 bedrooms and a den with a pull out couch where he slept.

To look at these two young gay men, it was difficult to tell that they were partners. Lenny was about six feet tall, very powerful. He worked out at the gym five days a week and had arms like a prize fighter. Charlie wasn't quite as tall or as muscular but he was always dressed to the nines, shined his shoes daily, wore black rimmed glasses and looked just like a college professor. If opposites really do attract, it was Charlie and Lenny.

"We'll be over at the house tomorrow morning about eight. Is that okay dad?"

Chapter 32

Saturday morning Katie arrived with her husband Joe and the two kids. It was before nine in the morning.

"Oh my gosh, Kate, how did you get here so early, all the way from the cape?" Olivia exclaimed as she gave her sister in law a big hug.

"Did you forget how early babies wake up, Livvy?" Katie laughed. Turning to face her mother, "Jess said they'd try to get here by ten, Mom. She'll bring her doctor with her to meet the rest of the family." Katie was almost silly about the new romance.

Bill, Charlie, Lenny and Donnie were unloading the truck. Joe went to help them. Olivia was directing where she wanted things to go. Katie and Emma began opening boxes and putting dishes and glasses into the dishwasher. Olivia had gone over to the house the day before and lined all of the shelves and began filling cabinets with cleaning supplies and paper products.

It was a beautiful day heading up into the high fifties so the children played out back in the fenced in yard. Ricky joined his cousins who he had not seen in over two years. The rain had washed away most of all the snow; the only remaining snow to be seen were the piles that had been shoveled or plowed on the sides of the road.

Just before ten o'clock Jessie and Clay arrived bringing donuts and Dunkin Donut coffees for everyone. Hugs and kisses went around the house once again. The truck was empty and it was a great time to take a break.

When everyone was gathered around the table and chairs that were so nicely placed by Olivia's helpers, Jessie asked for attention.

"I would like all of you to know that as of last evening, Clayton and I became engaged. I'm getting married!" She jumped up and down with excitement like a child, waving the two carat diamond ring on her left hand.

More hugs and kisses and shaking hands with congratulations. Jessie was beaming. Emma was a little surprised this was all happening so fast but Katie had tried to warn her it could be coming someday soon.

"I am so happy for you sweetheart." Emma hugged her

daughter.

"Mom, I'll be moving out of your house in the next few weeks so you can do what you need to get it ready to rent for the summer season. I'll pay to have it cleaned, of course, Mom."

"Have you set a date or thought about it yet, Jess?" Katie inquired.

"We are not going to have a big wedding and all that hoop-la. So we're just going to fly to some island and get married there, make it a honey moon wedding. Maybe in June."

Emma noticed the expression on Katie's face, she seemed to be disappointed that she wouldn't be involved in her sister's wedding. But Kate regained her composure and told her it sounded wonderful.

Just then, the front door opened. "Is anyone home?" A female voice called out.

It was Lucy and Molly, Bill's daughter and granddaughter. "We came to help and to see my dear brother." Lucy went to hug Charlie and then she hugged Lenny as well.

"You guys look so awesome. California definitely agrees with you. Oh Charlie, I've missed you so much." Lucy didn't know Lenny very well but she knew that he made her brother happy and that's all that anyone cared about.

After their coffee break the men began assembling beds and putting the drawers into the bureaus while the women hung curtains and pictures on the wall. It was a family affair.

Emma was in the kitchen doing what she does best, cooking. She brought bags of groceries with her and had lunch all planned out. She arranged a platter of cold cuts on the breakfast counter with hoagie rolls and condiments so they could make their own sandwiches. She had a jar of peanut butter and one of jelly and a loaf of bread to make PB&J's for the kids. Then she took down the small bowls that she had bought at Walmart's during the week as a contribution to Olivia's dishware. She turned off the stove and called out to all the busy bees.

"Who wants Momma's famous Clam Chowdah?" in her Cape Cod accent. She made it just the way her father had taught her back in the good ole deli days.

They all came running for lunch, mommies getting the children into the bathrooms to wash their hands and faces. Bill had taken the little table and chairs from their kitchen to bring to Donnie's new house and they pulled up two additional chairs from the low beach chairs that they had found stored in the basement.

Everyone was gathering around the table, chatting away, clanging bowls and glasses and getting comfortable with their delicious food. Donnie stood by the kitchen counter and he was silent. Emma noticed him standing alone without food.

"Donnie. Are you okay honey?" She feared he may have hurt himself moving something.

Silence filled the room. Even the children got quiet. Donnie reached for napkin on the table and wiped his tear filled eyes.

It took him a while to compose himself so that he'd be able to speak. Everyone was staring at him, unable to eat, waiting to see what he was going to say.

"How can I ever thank you? I can't believe it, but I'm HOME! Thank you Jesus. Thank you family. I love you all so very much." And he burst into tears and left the room.

"He'll be okay." Olivia said with a very soft voice. "He's just a bit overwhelmed at the moment. Ever since the surgery he has become very emotional, feeling very blessed at this new chance to live again. Go ahead and eat, I'll check on him."

A few minutes later, Donnie being Donnie returned, with a big smile on his face.

"Hey, I just wanted you all to be quiet. I was kidding. Where's the grub, I'm starved." He pulled up a chair and sat down. Emma stood up and smacked him on the side of the head, kiddingly.

"You are such a bratty son." Emma said before kissing his cheek. She then went to get him a bowl of chowder.

Chapter 33

Olivia woke up early the next morning and rolled over to hug her husband.

"You are awake early. Are you feeling okay honey?" She asked him quietly. It felt good to be in their own bed, in their new house.

"Yeah, I'm fine, Liv. I was just listening to the birds. It's Spring, ya know."

"You are too funny, Donovan Richard. Do you really listen to the birds?" Olivia looked into her husband's handsome face and found such serenity and peace. And he was breathing so easily. She gave a silent thanks to God and to the donor they never knew.

"Sure I listen to the birds. I do it all the time. Don't forget, I spent a great deal of time in bed at home and in the hospital. First thing in the morning before the sun comes up I listen to the sounds of silence and then I'll hear a little chirp here and there. Today there is a robin talking his head off and as the sun got a little brighter I heard a cardinal and then a few others chirped their morning songs. It's beautiful Liv." He turned to face her. "Just like you first thing in the morning. You are so beautiful. I love you Olivia. Thank you for sticking by me through all of this. You are a good wife and mother." He pulled her close and kissed her hard.

"Daddy, Daddy, can we come downstairs now?" Billy yelled from the top of the stairs.

Donnie looked at his wife and smiled. "Hold that thought. The wild Indians are up and at it already."

"Yes sport, come on down and come in here and give me a hug."

Donnie sat at the edge of his bed and his two kids ran into their parents' bedroom squealing with excitement to be in a new house. They wanted to go out to play.

"We need to eat breakfast first," Olivia told them, throwing on her bathrobe.

She took the kids out to the kitchen and let Donnie take his shower and shave.

The sun was bright and made the house feel fresh and alive.

Olivia was going to like living in this house. She was so grateful for all the help they had. They moved in and got set up all in one day now they were ready to unpack some more boxes and move on with their lives.

"AAHHH" Donnie yelled from the bathroom. Olivia ran to see what the problem was. "There's no hot water. I just stepped into the shower and it was freezing cold." Olivia laughed.

"I thought something was wrong, Donnie. I could smack you. Did you remember to turn on the hot water heater like Bill told you twice as he was leaving last night?"

Donnie smiled and shrugged his shoulders. "Guess I'll go turn on the hot water heater and have some breakfast before my shower." He kissed his wife and patted her behind as he walked by her in his pajama bottoms to go to the basement where the hot water tank was located.

"Put on a shirt, Donnie, and some slippers. You'll catch cold, Donovan!" Olivia called after him as he turned around to go back into their bedroom to do what he was told. He was smiling. She was always looking after him, like one of their kids. Yes indeed, he was a lucky man. He had a great wife.

Bill and Emma took Charlie and Lenny down to the Cape to see what they would do about fixing up the house Jessie was temporarily living in; Emma's house. Emma called Jess on her cell phone to say that they were on their way and asked if she needed anything. Jessie was over at Clay's house and said she'd meet them at the house. They would go out to lunch later.

Bill pulled into the driveway and Jessie had not yet arrived but Emma still had her key so they went inside. She just shook her head at the sight of the place. Jessica was NOT a good house keeper. Emma began picking up dirty laundry that was thrown around, and Charlie laughed. He knew Emma was perturbed.

"I wonder if Clayton has ever been invited here," he chuckled.

"I'm glad he's a doctor who can afford to hire a house maid. I could kill this kid of mine. She is such a slob."

At that outburst Jessie walked in the back door.

"Did I hear someone call my name?" She blushed as she too began picking up old newspapers and mail that had been strewn about. "Sorry guys," she said to Charlie and Lenny.

"Mom, I'm not a neatnik but I take care of things."

"Neatnik, Jessica Ann? You my dear daughter are the biggest messiest woman I know. I hope Clayton knows about this before he marries you."

"Oh, believe me Emma, I do know," Clay walked in the door carrying an armful of chopped wood for the fireplace. He walked over to the wood stove and started a fire to take the chill off.

"And he loves me anyway, Ma." Jess piped up hugging her fiancé.

The men walked around with a notebook and pen, checking for things that needed to be either repaired or replaced. Emma and Jessie tidied up the place a little and Jess threw a load of laundry into the washing machine, apologizing to her mother for the mess. "I've just been so busy Mom, working full time and then helping Donnie yesterday. I just didn't get a chance to clean up. I'm sorry." Her head tilted to one side like she was that little girl who disappointed her mother again and again.

The guys were all busy and getting into the crawl space and up on the roof and doing a thorough home inspection so Emma decided to run up to the market and pick up stuff for lunch, rather than have them stop in mid-stream to go out for lunch. She told Jessie to set the table and she'd be back in just a little while.

In the deli department they had hot fried chicken and sides of baked beans and macaroni and cheese. Ready to eat. Emma also bought some King Hawaiian dinner rolls to go with it. She picked up some butter to make sure, not trusting her daughter to have anything in the fridge. She was going down the soda aisle when she heard her name being called.

"Emma. Hello Emma." It was a warm friendly male voice that she thought she recognized.

She turned around and saw Jack Hynes walking towards her to give her a big hug.

"You look great Emma. What brings you to town? Visiting

your girls?"

"Hi Jack. Yes, my daughter Jessica is going to get married and we need to help her move out of my cottage. I'll probably rent it out for the season. So nice to see you."

Emma's face was a little flushed at bumping into this old boyfriend from years ago. She should have brushed her hair before she left the house, she was thinking, as she pushed her hair behind her ears. He looked so good.

"Daddy, Daddy." I little boy rounded the corner and ran into Jack's arms. He was followed by a lovely blonde pushing a grocery cart with a little blonde girl in the seat.

"Emma, I think you met my wife a few years ago, before she was my wife of course." He kind of tried to make a joke, feeling a bit awkward at the introduction.

"Pam this is Emma Clark. Oh excuse me, Emma, you remarried didn't you?"

Emma held out her hand to shake with the very pregnant Pam Hynes.

"I'm now Emma Jeffers. Nice to meet you Pam." His wife smiled politely.

"And this is my son, Jason, and my little girl Julie and we'll be having another little boy next month." Jack was so proud of his young family.

"I'm so happy for you Jack. You have a beautiful family." He knew she understood how happy he was. They had been good friends.

"By the way, thank you for helping Donnie." Emma referred to his large donation to Donnie's website but she wasn't sure how much his wife knew so she didn't want to say too much.

"Oh Emma, how is he doing now? He was going to move back east, has he arrived yet?"

Emma was a little shocked that he knew about Donnie moving home. She told him the update and thanked him again.

"I always had a soft spot for him, Emma. He's a fine young man. I did what I could to make his life better and any time he needs help, you just have him call me. He's got my number. Anything at all."

Emma thanked him again and said good bye to him and his

young family. She was puzzled that Jack knew so much and what did he mean by he did what he could to make his life better?

Emma didn't want the lunch food to get cold so she hurried along after she picked up a case of soda. The gang was eagerly waiting for her return, all washed up and seated around the extended table out on the patio warmed up by the electric heater. Jess had done a good job at setting the table with everything that was needed.

Emma pulled each carton out of the bags and placed it in the center of the table with the serving spoons and she went to wash her hands. She couldn't shake what Jack had said to her about helping Donnie. Surely he didn't send more than that thousand dollars? Or did he? She would call Donnie later when she was alone.

She returned to the table with the rest of the family and they all had a hot lunch.

As they were cleaning up Katie pulled into the driveway with her two kids.

"I called her while you were at the store and told her to come over while you were here." Jess told her mother.

"Hi darling," Emma hugged her daughter and took her granddaughter from her arms so Katie could take Ricky's coat and hat off.

"Go give Nana a big kiss, Ricky," Katie instructed her son, as she took her daughter back from grandma's arms to remove her snowsuit.

"Katie, the baby is sweating honey. That snowsuit is too warm for her now. We'll need to get her some pretty pink spring clothes." Nana kissed little Molly. "Jessie go get a wet facecloth for the baby, let's wash her cute little face. She is still so tiny, isn't she?"

"Oh yeah." Katie said. "She's all girl, tiny and feminine. So different from her big brother. And yet she eats all the time. I have to supplement my breast milk with formula because I can't keep her satisfied." Katie told her mother while Auntie Jess wiped the little girl's face and cooed to her.

"Katie, why don't you leave your pediatrician and come to us? Clay is such a great doctor." Jess asked her sister.

"Well I didn't know Clayton when Ricky was born and since

I've been going to Dr. Johnson for four years now, I didn't see any reason to switch."

"Well it's easy to switch over, Katie. I can get you the paper work. All you have to do it sign it and bring it to your doctor's office. They'll send all the medical records over to our office. You don't have to do anything else. Katie, we can save you money on office visits and give you free samples when you need something. Think about it, okay?" Jess begged her sister. She took Molly into her arms and bounced her up and down.

"I wouldn't do that, Jessie. I just fed her before we came over. She might vomit all over you." Katie was laughing. "Joe got up in the middle of the night to feed her a few days ago and she peuked all over him. He swore and yelled for me to come get her before he started to vomit. That was the end of him helping me, I guess." She laughed again. "She is just so delicate. He's used to rough housing with Ricky, he can't deal with her just yet."

They all sat around talking, telling Emma what needed to be done to the house and they decided who they would contact as a realtor to show the cottage for rent. By four o'clock, Bill and Emma and the boys were on their way home to Manomet. It had been a full but fulfilling day. They got a lot accomplished and Emma got to see her grandchildren.

Emma never found a chance to call Donnie to talk about meeting Jack. She decided she'd wait until the right opportunity presented itself, and yet she tossed and turned all night wondering what it was that he told her, to make her feel so unsettled. It was almost as if he thought she knew what he was talking about but didn't want to say anything in front of his wife, but for the life of her, Emma had no clue what he meant.

Monday morning Donnie left the house to go meet his old, now renewed, boss, Jason. He wasn't ready to get back to work full time just yet, however he was ready to get acquainted with what his job would entail and where he'd be working. Jason had told him he could start slow, a few hours a day until he was well enough to tackle the position. Donnie still had to go to Boston to meet with his new doctor and get set up with his new medical plan here.

Emma had given her car to Charlie and Lenny to go play tourist and go see Plymouth Rock in the harbor and do some sightseeing. It had been a number of years since they were back home. Plymouth was a beautiful place in the spring with many nice restaurants and sights to see. It was their day to relax and enjoy themselves.

Bill had gone to his office and checked with Scott, his son-in-law-foreman. He needed to go over a few things with him and make plans for doing the renovations to Emma's house on the Cape.

Emma was home alone without a car so she decided to sit down at the computer and check in with Facebook and see what was happening with Donnie's website. She was surprised that it had been discontinued without her knowledge. He had exceeded his goal and time ran out and the website was closed down. She made a mental note to call Donnie and ask him if he knew about it. Of course he knew about it. They had been living from those donations. It would be a good excuse to call him, anyway, she thought, and somehow tell him about running into Jack Hynes.

Emma called his cell and it went to voice mail. Instead of leaving a message, she sent him a text asking him to call her when he was available. He replied to her text, at work, will call later. She smiled at his reply. "At work". Wonderful words. Donnie hadn't been able to work for almost three years.

Bill came home mid-afternoon and found his wife sitting on the floor in the kitchen. "What are you doing on the floor, Emma?" He laughed, as he helped her up.

She told him she decided to organize the cleaning supplies under the cabinet.

It's been so hectic with so much going on lately then all of a sudden everyone was off or busy and I found I had time on my hands so I tackled something I wanted to do since we moved it. Everything just got thrown under the sink. I needed to organize it," she explained. He kissed her forehead.

"What are you making for dinner?" Bill sat down at the kitchen counter and opened the mail. He was just making small talk as things were slowly getting back to normal again. Other than having house guests for a few more days.

"I am making reservations," she joked in reply. "Seriously, Bill. Let's take the boys to dinner at Tinker's Dam. We haven't been there for ages. I love that place."

"It's kind of romantic, Emma. Do think it's appropriate to bring the boys there?"

Emma was a little surprised at his response. "Bill. It is a lovely quaint place with a harpist in the lounge. It might be romantic for us but it is just such a special place. I thought you might like to share it with your son and his special friend. They aren't really KIDS anymore, Bill. " Emma never held any reservations against his son for being gay. He loved her for that.

Even with reservations for seven thirty, they had to wait for a table. Some restaurants were closed on Mondays because they were so slow but the Inn was a very popular spot. She had been lucky to get reservations on such short notice.

They sat in the lounge with the young female harpist playing popular tunes. There were candles on all of the small cocktail tables and the room was dimly lit. Maybe Bill had been right, Emma thought, it is rather a romantic atmosphere, but then she looked at Charlie and Lenny and saw that they were thoroughly enjoying it as well.

Emma sipped her cosmopolitan and sighed. Bill looked at her and smiled back.

"You have a lovely smile on your face, Mrs. Jeffers. Are you enjoying yourself?" Emma nodded.

"This is a great place, Emma. Thank you for taking us here. I hope the food is as wonderful as the atmosphere and the drinks. Just look at this chocolate martini." Lenny picked up his nine ounce glass to show it off then sipped and aahhhed. They all smiled.

Bill sat up a little straighter in his chair and held up his single malted scotch on the rocks. "I'd like to offer my gratitude to you two wonderful young men. Thank you for all that you've done to help Donnie and his family." They all clinked glasses.

"Thank you from the bottom of my heart," Emma added.

"Charlie I am so proud of the man that you have become. I love you, son." Bill looked right into his son's face with so much love and pride. Charlie's eyes filled with tears.

"Thanks Dad," Charlie said, choking on his words. "My whole life all I ever wanted to do was to make you proud of me." He was speaking softly but it certainly got Bill's attention.

"When I was a kid, I didn't want to play little league baseball and I knew you were disappointed. You were a fireman, a real man's man. Do you know how long I kept my personal feelings from you, hoping you'd never learn who I was inside? I loved you, Dad. No, I worshipped you and all I ever did was disappoint you. Don't say anything. Just listen to me please." Charlie composed himself and looked at everyone at the table.

"I knew I could never be the son that you wanted. I tried. But it wasn't in me. I worked with you and you taught me a trade and I respected you for it, but I wasn't as good as the other guys. I knew you wanted me to do better. Scott is a master at woodworking. I'm good at sitting at a computer and engineering how something should go together and I can assemble things, but I work more with my head than my hands. The hardest thing I ever had to do was look into your face the day I told you that I was gay. Your suspicion was confirmed and the total let down rushed in. I saw that final disappointment in your expression. You couldn't say one word. You just hung your head."

Charlie looked around the room to make sure no one was listening to him talk. They were all engaged in their own conversations.

"For you to tell me today that you are proud of me, that you love me, is the best day of my life. All of my life all I ever wanted you to tell me was that you were proud of something I did. And today you say you are proud of who I AM. That's huge, Dad."

Tears fell from not only Charlie's eyes but from everyone one of them at the table. Charlie stood up at the same time his father rose from his chair and they hugged in a warm, loving, tearful embrace.

"I regret not having told you before now, Charlie. I've always been proud of you, son."

Just then, saved by the bell came to mind when the host came in to bring the Jeffers party to their table for dinner. Beverage napkins were grabbed to dab at the teary eyes as they followed the maitre d' into the dining room, to their table by the huge fireplace.

Chapter 34

Wednesday evening, Donnie and Olivia invited Charlie and Lenny, and Bill and Emma over the house for a spaghetti feed. Donnie made his own homemade sauce with Italian sausages and Olivia made her garlicky meat-a-balls, as Donnie called them. Emma said she'd bring dessert and she made chocolate covered chewy brownies and brought the vanilla bean ice cream.

Donnie and Olivia wanted to thank Charlie and Lenny for everything they had done for them and since the guys were flying back to California in the morning, cooking dinner for them was the least they could do.

Lenny said he'd make an antipasto the way his Italian grandma once taught him. He liked to cook. So he brought in the bag of groceries and went right to the kitchen where he made himself at home chopping and slicing.

Emma brought a few bottles of red wine and some crusty bread along with dessert. They sat around drinking and eating and laughing and then when it was time to go, the two guys gave Olivia a big hug and kissed her good bye. Charlie pulled Donnie into a gentlemanly hug, careful not to squeeze too hard, and wished him luck. They had grown quite fond on one another. Lenny shook his hand and patted his shoulder.

"Good Luck man. You are one brave soul and I commend you, brother." He said to Donnie. "If you ever need anything, you just call me, ya hear?"

Thursday morning Bill drove his son and Lenny to Logan airport to catch the first plane to Los Angeles. It had been foggy when they first got on the highway but by the time they reached the airport, the fog had lifted and their plane was "on time".

Over the next few weeks Olivia got the children enrolled in preschool and signed up for kindergarten which they would attend in September. They were almost five years old. Donnie had his first appointment with his new doctor and all of his tests were good. Jessie had moved out of the cottage and in with her fiancé. Katie had transferred her children's medical records over to Dr. Clayton Drake's office. And her first appointment was scheduled for the following week.

Bill had gone down to the cape with Scott and one other employee to begin work on Emma's beach cottage. The realtor had stopped by to take pictures and list the property for rent for the upcoming summer season.

Saturday morning Donnie's cell phone rang. It was his sister Jess.

"Are you super busy today? I need to talk to you. Just you. One on one." Jessie sounded serious.

"Sure, Jess, do you want to come up here or meet someplace?"

"Can you meet me at the Ninety Nine in Norwell? It's just off the highway. You can get some lunch or something. Can you make it by eleven thirty?"

Donnie told her it wasn't a problem, he'd be there for her. Jessie never asked him for anything, ever. He was concerned that something was wrong.

She was on her second cup of coffee when Donnie arrived at eleven twenty. She said there had been no traffic leaving the cape so she made good time. She refused anything to eat, saying she wasn't feeling very well, but told him to order something. He ordered the open faced hot roast beef sandwich with mashed potatoes and gravy. Jessie smiled.

"You've still got that big appetite, I see." She teased him.

"I need to consume over two thousand calories a day just to hold my weight were it is. More if I want to gain weight, which I need to do. The doctor said I should gain about ten pounds more if I can. It's not as easy as it sounds for someone with CF."

Jessie nodded and looked down. She didn't know quite how to begin.

"What's up Jess? What can I do to help you, whatever it is?" Donnie said.

"Well Donnie." She started and stopped to gather her thoughts, even though she rehearsed what she was going to say on her ride up from the cape.

"We are going to move our wedding date up. We made arrangements to go to St. Lucia on May 8th and get married that

Saturday on the 9th."

"Well, that's great, but what does it have to do with me, Jessie?" Donnie didn't understand what she was so upset about.

"We talked about doing it in June but then, well, I'm pregnant, Donnie." Her eyes filled with tears and she had a sad smile on her face.

"Isn't that a good thing, Jess? You said you guys want a couple of kids, right?"

Donnie remembered his mother telling him that Jess might not be able to have children as she has had several miscarriages. He thought maybe perhaps she was nervous about losing another child. And her age was becoming a factor.

"Oh Donnie, yes. We do. In fact I stopped taking the pill over a month ago and we said if I got pregnant it wouldn't matter. I'm not getting any younger, time's a wasting. So we kinda like planned it, ya know?" Donnie nodded waiting for the other shoe to drop.

"Donnie, we went to get our marriage license and we needed to take a blood test." She swallowed hard and took a sip of her cold coffee. "Donnie, both Clay and I are carriers of the CF gene." Crocodile tears puddled in her eyes and slid down her cheeks.

"Whoa," said Donnie, sitting up straight in the booth.

Just then, his lunch was delivered. "Can I get you anything else, sir?" the server asked him. He shook his head, unsure of his voice at that moment.

The server warmed Jessie's coffee and asked her if she wanted anything else.

"No. No, thank you, we're all set." Jess replied sweetly.

"Okay." Started Donnie, neglecting to touch his food. "I'm sure you know the statistics. One in four. You have a twenty five percent chance of having a baby with Cystic Fibrosis is you are both carriers. You know that, right?" Donnie questioned Jess.

He cut up his meat and took a bite followed by some mashed potatoes, then took a big drink of water.

"You can have *Amniocentesis* performed to see if you are carrying a child with a disease. You know that too, right?"

"I know that Donnie. But I had more than one miscarriage in

my life. I was afraid I might not even be able to get pregnant. What if I aborted it and then never could conceive again? I'd never forgive myself. I want this baby, Donnie, but I don't want my child to have to suffer his whole life like you have. It just isn't fair to the child. I don't know what to do Donnie." Jess was fighting back the tears. She had cried all night long. She didn't want to make a spectacle of herself in the restaurant.

Donnie ate a few more bites. Jess knew he was thinking what to say to her.

"Jess. I'm not sure what you think I can do or say to help you decide what to do. If you want me to tell you it's okay to have a kid with CF, I can't do that. If I knew I was going to bring a child into the world with this horrible disease, I would not do it. But I don't know if I could abort it either. You know my religion is strong, so I can't tell you to go ahead and get rid of it. Yes, I have suffered my whole life. It has not been an easy journey. But look at me. I have new lungs now. I can breathe. I can drive a car. I can get a job. I have a wife and two beautiful children." And there, he stopped abruptly.

He put his fork down. Took a sip of water and looked into his sister's eyes.

"Okay. I know what I need to tell you. Not that it will help you decide but it's True Confession time. Jessie, I'm swearing you to secrecy. Mom doesn't even know."

The server returned to check to see if his customers needed anything. No thanks.

"Well you know that Liv and I tried for years to have a baby, right? You do know how badly we wanted kids, right Jessie?" He wanted her full attention.

"Well we tried everything, or so we thought. I just don't have a good sperm count. I don't have any sperm count. I was finally told that I would never be able to get my wife pregnant. I was crushed. She was devastated. It wasn't her, it was me. Talk about feeling like a failure. I hated this disease so much on that day." He took another drink.

"Do you remember Mom's friend Jack Hynes?" Jess nodded that she did.

"He was like another Charlie. He came to my rescue. I truly

believe that God sends you angels when you are in need of help. He came to our house one day and told us about a doctor he knew personally. He explained about artificial insemination, which we had already tried and failed due to my lack of sperm."

Donnie stopped, not sure how to continue without divulging the secret he and Olivia had kept for five years.

"Jessie. Jack Hynes donated his sperm so that Liv could get pregnant." There. It was out. He said it. Now he was letting his sister digest what he had just confessed.

"So, Jack Hynes is really the biological father of your children?" Jess asked timidly.

"Actually, yes. But he did it all legal. Went to a sperm bank. Signed a waiver. He would never look for anything regarding the baby. And he paid for every cent of it. Liv had been injected with his sperm three times before she got pregnant and as it turned out, we had twins due to the hormones that she had been taking to help her get pregnant."

Jess sat motionless for a moment and then she smiled."What a beautiful story, Donnie. And you never told Mom?" Donnie shook his head.

"I never told anyone. Neither has Olivia. Just you. And how that helps you, I don't know, but I just wanted to let you know how badly we wanted kids. And we had no idea if the babies she carried would be diseased, deformed or carry an illness. We were ready to deal with anything at that point. We felt that our love would get us through it. But God blessed us with two beautiful, healthy children and Jack remains a close friend to this day. He set up a trust fund for my kids when they were born. Any time I need anything for the kids, I have the right to borrow from it, but it goes to them when they turn twenty one."

It was Jessie's turn to say 'Whoa'.

As it sunk in, Jess began to think. "But the kids look just like you guys. They've got their mother's light blonde hair and your dark eyes, your coloring?" It was more of a question than a statement.

"Do you remember Jack, Jessie? He has sandy colored hair and brown eyes." Donnie smiled. They had similar traits.

"Donnie, you have no idea how much you have helped me by sharing that story. I will probably have the Amnio, but even if the child has CF or Downs, I won't abort it. I will just take precautions and be prepared to take good care of it and love it to the best of my ability. I love you so much Donnie. Calling you was the best thing in the world." She threw him a kiss across the table.

"Go ahead and finish your lunch. It's getting cold." She smiled at him as he picked up his fork to dig in.

"What do you say to a party tomorrow if I can get everyone together on short notice? I want to let everyone know that I am going to have Clayton's baby and we're getting married on May 9th. Will you come? Will you be there for me, moral support?"

"Will you serve food?" he teased her. "Of course I'll be there with my family. We can make it a birthday party. The twins turn five tomorrow."

Chapter 35

It was the first time the family was invited to Dr. Clay's house in Chatham. It wasn't a huge house but it was lovely, over looked a knoll with the water far below. It was a little too chilly with the breeze off the bay so they cooked steaks on the grill outside but they ate inside.

Emma made her out-of-this-world potato salad. Katie had gone to the farmer's market and bought fresh corn on the cob. Donnie and Olivia brought a box of Kraft Mac & Cheese for the kids, some watermelon and a birthday cake.

They ate and they talked and they ate some more and sang happy birthday to Billy and Beth. They let the kids open their gifts. Nana was smart, she also brought a gift for Ricky so he wouldn't feel left out.

And then Jessie asked for everyone's attention for her announcement.

"I brought you all here on the pretense that it was just for the twins' birthday but I'd also like to tell you that Clay and I," and she reached for her fiancé's hand. "We are going to have a baby. I'm six weeks pregnant. We are flying to St. Lucia and getting married on May 9th. It's just a short few days but our work schedule wouldn't permit us to take off very long. We're very truly blessed to share this wonderful news with all of you. Thank you for coming on short notice." Clay stood and kissed her as everyone applauded.

Right on queue little Miss Molly began to cry to be fed.

"Here, let me hold her while you get her bottle warmed up, Kate." Donnie took the baby from his sister. He began to walk around with her, talking to her in his soft daddy voice. He kissed her little rosy cheek. He patted her head. Bounced her up and down. He took her tiny hand in his and played with her fingers.

Emma walked up behind him. "Maybe she needs her diaper changed, Donnie. Bring her into the bedroom and I'll change her."

"Ma." Donnie spoke in almost a whisper when they were alone in the bedroom.

"Ma." He repeated to get Emma's attention. "Have you kissed this child before?"

"Well of course. That's a silly question. Why?"

"Kiss her now, Ma." Donnie placed the child on the bed to be diaper changed.

Emma leaned over and kissed her. She looked at Donnie. The baby continued to cry hard. Emma picked up her granddaughter and kissed her again.

"Oh Donnie. I never noticed."

Donnie took her tiny hand in his and showed his mother the baby's fingers. They were clubbed like his were. He felt her stomach and it was as hard as a rock.

"She isn't hungry mom. Molly is starving." Emma began to cry as she rocked the little girl in her arms.

"Oh God no, Donnie. It can't be happening again."

"Hey you two," Katie came to the room with the bottle in her hand.

"What's wrong, Ma?" Katie looked worried as she saw her mother's tears.

Donnie took the bottle from his sister's hand and grabbed the child from his mother's arms and left the room to feed Molly. He closed the door on his way out so that his mother could speak privately to Kate.

"Katie, did you ever have Molly tested?" Emma didn't know how to ask the question.

"Tested for what, Ma? For what? CF? Oh Ma, don't even go there."

"Katie, she has all the symptoms. Molly needs to be tested."

"Mom. You and Donnie just think everyone has the disease. Just leave us alone okay?" Katie stormed out of the bedroom to retrieve her child. She was in denial.

"Joe, help Ricky put his coat on please. We have leave, right now, please." Katie was trembling. Her husband looked at her like she had rocks in her head but he knew her tone of voice meant for him not to ask questions.

Jess went up to Donnie as Katie pulled her daughter away from him, putting the bottle back in the child's mouth.

"Katie, what's up?" Jess asked, looking from her brother to her sister. She thought they had a fight but then Emma walked out of the bedroom, wiping her tears with a tissue.

At that precise moment the baby had to vomit and the projectile vomiting went across the room soaking everything in its path. Katie was reduced to tears and began to crumble.

Everyone went to help. Emma took the baby into the other room to clean her off and change her. Jessie grabbed her sister by the shoulders and helped her to a chair where she sobbed.

"I've been thinking that there was something wrong for weeks now. I just can't handle it. It can't be. Oh God please no." Katie almost screamed with fear and hurt.

Jess looked up at Donnie. "What's going on Donnie?"

"Ma and I think maybe Molly should be tested for Cystic Fibrosis."

The room became so silent you couldn't hear a sound, only Katie's cries.

"Kiss her, Jessie. She tastes salty. Look at her clubbed fingers. They are tiny so it's easy to miss. See how hard her distended stomach is? She isn't getting nourishment from her food so that's why she is still so tiny. She isn't growing even though she is eating like crazy. She is starving to death, literally. And that little cold? Listen to her chest. She's wheezing. She has all of the signs. Katie is too close to see it, perhaps. But they are there. Molly needs a sweat test to see if she has CF." Donnie declared what they all neglected to see.

"If she had brought the baby to Clay he would've discovered it before now. I tried to convince her. I knew in my heart something was wrong and not being done." Jess was so upset. Clayton put his arm around her.

"We know about Donnie so we'd be more apt to find it, to look for the signs. Maybe Kate's pediatrician doesn't know about the family history. Don't judge him. I just feel badly that we didn't see it before now but then again, how often have we been around the baby?"

Joe stood up after putting his son's jacket on. He had been silent until now.

"You mean to tell me that you think our little girl is sick, like you?" He just could not comprehend this whole situation. He was dumb struck. Everyone looked at him with sympathy.

"It'll be okay, Joe. They have some good treatments today. Hey, she hasn't been tested yet, maybe I'm off base." Donnie was trying to sound positive.

Joe helped his wife with the children and they left but not before she gave Donnie a silent hug. She told Jessie to arrange the test ASAP. She left in tears. Joe was angry.

"I'm so sorry Jessie. I guess I ruined your good news and the party. I just couldn't believe what I was seeing. You have to know what to look for, and I surely know what it's like to have all the symptoms. I feel bad that it had to be me, though." Donnie said sadly.

Emma drove down to the cape to go to the doctor with Katie when she was to have Molly tested. Katie called her in tears asking her to go with her. She was scared and Joe was no help. He flat out refused to go with her. He just couldn't face it; he was in total denial. Kate told her mother that he had been drinking heavily since the party.

The test confirmed what they all now believed to be true.

Molly had Cystic Fibrosis.

"Life expectancy today, Kate, is into their mid thirties. It is still *incurable.* However, look at your brother. He was given fourteen years to live and he's already into his mid thirties with new lungs and a new lease on life. By the time Molly reaches his age, there will probably be a cure and she'll be living a full life. In the meantime…" he went on to tell her what they needed to do.

On the ride home, Kate was very quiet. Emma drove.

"Mom. We've been preoccupied with Molly lately but how do you think Jessie is feeling about being pregnant? Did she tell you that both she and Clay carry the defective gene? She could have a child with CF as well."

Emma almost drove off the road. Jessie had not told her mother that she was a carrier. Things just happened too quickly and Jess never had the opportunity.

"Sorry, Mom. I thought she told you." Kate felt badly for spilling the beans.

That evening after dinner, Emma went into the living room and made a call to her oldest daughter. "Kate told me that you and Clay are carriers of CF."

Jessie apologized for not having told her herself but she went on to say how she met with Donnie and how he enlightened her. She was going to have this baby no matter what. She had been sick with morning sickness every day and if she could live through that, she could do anything, she joked with her mother, trying to lighten the air.

Jess went on to tell Emma that Dr. Clay found a good doctor in Boston that will take Molly on as a new patient. Donnie's CF doctor only cared for adults that had transplants. Donnie was medically coded as PT, post transplant, and no longer as CF. They were like two different diseases. All the doctors today specialized in different levels of medicine.

Jess said that she was so happy she talked Katie into transferring from her old pediatrician so now she would have access to Molly's medical records and could help her sister more. It was a good conversation and Emma was glad she made the call.

"Join me in a cup of herbal tea, sweetheart?" she asked Bill who was dozing in front of the television.

"Only if you have something yummy to go with it," he replied, turning off the set.

"I made an apple crisp that I took to Katie's today, but I saved a piece just for you." She smiled at him as they walked into the kitchen, hand in hand.

Chapter 36

Jessie sat at the edge of the examining table. Her OB/GYN had just examined her.

"Everything is going along just fine, Jessica. Since you had the *Amniocentesis* everything has just gone along according to plan. I'm so happy for you and your husband that it all came out normal." The doctor was reviewing her chart as he spoke to her.

"Have you chosen a name for your little girl yet?"

"Yes. Jillian Marie. We'll call her Jilli. I don't like plain Jill, so I want something a little different for my baby girl. My husband is afraid they'll call her Jelly instead," and her doctor chuckled, "but I like Jilli. I think it's pretty," Jess said smiling proudly.

"Now it says here that your due date is in just four more weeks but often times, the first delivery goes past that date so don't be concerned if you don't go into labor right on time. It's all normal. Why don't we have you come back to see me in three weeks and I should be able to give you a closer due date?"

He helped Jess get up off the table and they exchanged

pleasantries. Jessie was all belly. From behind no one would know she was going to have a baby next month but from the front, you knew it wasn't going to be a small infant, she was huge. She waddled when she walked, often placing her hand at the base of her stomach for support.

She scheduled her next appointment and walked out into the parking lot to find that the sunny day had turned damp and cool. A crack of thunder warned her to get to her car before the rain began.

Good ole New England weather, Jessie was thinking…if you don't like the weather now, wait five minutes, and it will change. She chuckled to herself, remembering what her sister always said. She was in great spirits.

Her mother was having a little family get together on Sunday as she so often did, keeping her children and grandchildren around her, to keep a close watch on how everyone was doing without going to their houses.

Donnie was coming along very well, going into Boston for checkups every three months. Soon it would be every six months. He loved his job and Olivia was working about twenty five hours a week, mostly from home, doing bookkeeping chores. Their finances were getting to a normal, livable level. Their twins were thriving, making friends and going to school. Emma couldn't be happier for them, knowing they were blessed.

Katie was struggling with little Molly but she was handling it. Ricky was doing great; he was the big brother who was a big help to Kate. It was Joe that Emma was concerned about. Ever since his daughter was diagnosed, he hasn't been able to kick the drinking habit again. He had been sober for a long time before then. Emma knew it was hard on Katie but she rarely complained. She was too busy caring for her children.

Jess and her doctor husband were on top of the world. They were both CF carriers but they were about to have their first child, and after being tested, they knew they had won this hand. They agreed that they would not push the envelope by trying to have another child. God was granting them this one healthy child, without Cystic Fibrosis, so they would be satisfied. It was a pact they made with one another before they got the test results. "Please dear Lord, let this baby be free of any dreadful diseases, and I promise I'll not take the chance of having another baby," she prayed. Daily. And He listened to and answered her prayers.

Even though she couldn't stay on her feet all day, Jess still worked a few hours at the practice. They brought in another nurse that would take over for her once the baby came. She was teaching the new girl the ropes for the next few weeks then she would bow out and relax and prepare the nursery, which was practically all set up. Knowing it was a girl, they painted the room in a soft lavender and Jessie stenciled her name, Jillian, across the wall, over the frilly crib.

The staff at work had given her a baby shower a few weeks before so there was little left that she needed. In her time off to prepare, she'd wash all the little nighties and onesies and outfits. Put them away into the bureau that matched the crib. For now they were piled on top of the matching changing table.

Her head was full of delight and happy thoughts as she drove home in the rain as her baby girl kicked her from inside.

Chapter 37

Joe's cell phone rang and he swore. He knew it was his wife
before he checked the ID. "Hello Katie Did" he greeted her using his
playful name for her. He knew she would not be in a good mood.

"Joey, where the hell are you? You said you would be home
early from work today so I could go do my errands. God damn it, Joe."
Katie seldom swore.

"I know honey. I'm so sorry," his words were slurred. "I
stopped for a beer and ran into Jess's old boyfriend Brad and we got
playing a game of darts and…," Kate interrupted his excuse.

"I don't want to hear it, Joe. Are you coming home or do I
have to come get you again?" Katie hated it when he drove home
drunk. She reminded him that he had a family to support. They needed
him. "How many beers did you have, Joe?"

"Hmm I don't know, we were drinking pitchers," his words
faded as he reflected on his bad behavior.

"Okay. Listen to me, Joe. Karen just got off the bus from
school. I saw her go into her house. I'll have her come over here to

watch the kids and I'll come to get you. You better be outside waiting for me in ten minutes because you don't want me to go inside after you, do you, Joe?" It was a threat and he knew it. It pissed him off when she talked to him like that but he knew he was wrong.

"I'll be outside babe, sorry." He was always sorry afterward. Katie was so tired of it. She disconnected and made a call to her neighbor's daughter to babysit for half an hour.

"Hey Brad, um, I gotta go." He felt like a jerk in front of the guys when his wife treated him like a failure.

"Yeah yeah. I know. You pansy. I'll give you a ride home instead of her coming, Joe. You know that. Why have her come? Don't you feel like an asshole?" His friend did not understand. Brad had no wife to go home to. He had no one waiting for him at home.

"You shouldn't drive either, Brad," Joe tried to tell him. "Katie will drive you home, wait here with me." Brad laughed at him as he pulled the keys from his pocket and walked to his pickup truck.

"It's Friday, Brad. We don't have to work tomorrow. We can come back to get our trucks tomorrow and finish that game of darts."

Joe kept trying to get his friend to leave with him and not drive home but he failed. No one ever thinks they are THAT drunk.

Brad drove off and Joe sat on the top step outside waiting for Katie. It was raining but there was an overhang of the roof so he didn't get wet. Well not too wet. The spray helped to sober him up just a bit.

Brad revved up the truck and was laughing at Joe sitting on the step when he squealed out of the parking lot, going way too fast.

He thought he was a smart guy by taking all the side roads, avoiding the main streets where the cops might see him. He wasn't concentrating on driving, he was thinking about his friend Joe who was pussy whipped. Some days Brad felt lonely. He used to live with Jessie then he lived with another gal. When she threw him out, he moved into a winterized one bedroom cottage. When his friends were off doing holidays with their wives and kids it was tough being alone but today he was very happy that he could go home to his own little cottage and not have to listen to a woman nagging him. Poor Joe. His wife was so demanding and to be stuck home with that sick kid. His son was pretty cool though. Joe took him along many times but now the wife wouldn't let Ricky go with him, because Joe was drinking again. Brad sure did miss Joe when he was sober and staying home. He was glad to have his pal back again, to shoot darts and have a few brewskies after work.

The rain was coming down pretty heavy now and the wind had picked up. Brad never saw the stop sign and went sailing through it at forty miles per hour. He was dead on arrival at the Cape Cod Hospital at four thirty that rainy afternoon.

Chapter 38

"Excuse me, Doctor, but you have an emergency call on line two," the receptionist buzzed in over the intercom of the examining room where Clay was tending to a new patient. He hated to be interrupted and his receptionist knew it so it had to be a real emergency for her to call him.

Dr. Drake excused himself and went to his office to take the call. First he buzzed the front desk. "Roberta, whose calling?"

"It's the hospital doctor. They said it was an emergency for you."

Clay Drake thanked his receptionist who had been with him from the beginning when he set up this practice. She was a loyal employee.

"This is Dr. Drake. Can I help you?" He answered line two.

Clay's face went ashen when the person responded. His stomach flipped over and the room began to spin. He took several deep breaths then told them he'd be there shortly.

"Roberta, I need to leave. Please reschedule," his voice drifted into a sob as he hung up the phone. She ran to his office to check on him.

"Doctor, what's wrong? What happened?" Roberta asked him, closing his office door behind her.

He reached for a tissue and wiped his eyes.

"My wife was in an accident. Jessie is unconscious and needs surgery. I need to get to her. Can you….?" He couldn't finish his question.

"GO. Just Go. I'll take care of everything here. Oh, what about Mrs. Jackson in room three? Were you done with the exam?" He filled her in on what needed to be done saying his nurse could finish it up. It was time for the new employee to step it up.

He ran out the back door so the people in his waiting room wouldn't see him falling apart with worry about his wife and their unborn child.

Being a doctor on the Cape, everyone knew him at the hospital. He had privileges and they took him right to the doctor who took care of his wife when the ambulance brought her in.

"What happened?" was all Clay could ask the doctor, tears still in his eyes.

"A drunk went through a stop sign and broadsided her. She never saw him coming. She was conscious when the paramedics arrived but she blacked out on the way. We have her being prepped for surgery now. I'm sorry, Dr. Drake, but she's losing a lot of blood. We need to take the baby before it's too late. Her OB doctor is on the way."

Clay fell into a chair to catch his breath. "May I see her?"

"Of course, but she's unconscious. Perhaps you should make a call to her parents." His suggestion had never entered Clay's mind. She had an accident. Why call them now? He'd call when she woke up and was recovering. Unless…he couldn't complete that thought. This was not happening. Oh God, he prayed as he ran to see her.

"Emma." Dr. Clay was on his cell, pacing in the waiting room. "I am so sorry for this call but Jessie's been in an accident. She is in surgery. Emma," he choked, stumbling over the words he needed to say. "They don't know if Jessie will make it. They are taking the baby by C-section." He broke down and cried out loud over the phone.

Chapter 39

Donnie, Emma, and Bill gathered around to support Clay. The baby was doing fine but only weighed four pounds ten ounces. She was being monitored in the NICU; the. Neonatal intensive care unit. The doctors were working on Jessie.

Katie came running into the waiting room to greet them.

"I am so sorry it took me so long to get here." It was evident that she had been crying. "How is Jessie?" No one spoke, just shook their heads. No one knew what to say.

"How did it happen? Where was she when she got hit?" Katie had not been filled in with the details. She had been out shopping once she got Joe settled with the kids. When she got home from shopping, Joe was asleep in his recliner, snoring to beat the band. Fortunately the children were not in any harm.

She put away her groceries and fed the kids and started cooking supper when Joe woke up. He sluggishly walked up behind her, put his arms around her and said he was sorry again. He had slept off his drunken stupor and now he was ashamed. It was the same thing over and over.

"You know, Joe." Katie turned from the stove to face him. "I am getting pretty tired of these 'I'm sorrys'. One of these days I'm going to say it too, when I pack your bags and throw you out. You need to get help. You need to stop drinking. I cannot go on like this, Joe. I need a husband to be there to help me with the children." She was in a rare lecture form when she saw his face change.

"What?" Katie asked.

"Your mother called. Your sister was in an accident. I'm sorry, I should have called your cell but," Katie stopped him mid-sentence.

"What happened Joe? What did my mother say?"

"She said to meet her at the emergency room. Oh gosh, I forgot to call you. I fell asleep."

"You stupid ass, Joe. You didn't fall asleep. You freaking passed out. You are a no good drunk, Joe. I'm sick and tired of it. This is it. The final straw. You either get help or you are outa here. Do you hear me?" Katie was screaming and the baby began to cry.

Katie grabbed her purse and her cell phone. "Get your own

God Damned dinner. I'm going to the hospital." She slammed the door and left him with the crying children.

Donnie walked his sister out into the hall away from the others to answer her questions. Clay didn't need to hear it all over again. They walked together to the end of the corridor and stood by a window. It was still raining. It was dark and dreary and almost night fall.

"Jessie had gone to see her GYN today. She was on her way home in the rain when some drunk went thru a stop sign and smashed into her. Her car went round in circles and slammed into a tree on the opposite side to the street. She hit her head on the side window and her stomach on the steering wheel then the air bag smashed into her face. They said that the driver of the other car died on the way to the hospital. He reeked of booze. It was over on Walnut Street, only two miles from Jessie's house. Just two miles from home and she's all messed up. She was covered in blood; they had to take the baby. For being premature, she's a decent size. She'll be fine." Some consolation.

"Oh my God, Donnie. Oh my God." Katie covered her face with her hands and cried.

"The baby is going to be okay, Katie." He repeated. "She's small but they think she's going to be fine. Clay checked her over too. She'll be okay, Katie." Donnie thought his sister was freaking out about them having to take the baby prematurely.

"Donnie. Oh God, Donnie. I bet that drunk driver was Joe's friend, Jessie's old boyfriend, Brad. Joe had been drinking all afternoon with him at the Hitching Post, just up the street from Walnut. Brad was on his way home. I had to go pick Joe up because he was too trashed to drive, again. Oh dear Lord, I hope it wasn't Brad who caused this." Katie was shaking. Donnie pulled her into a hug.

"Katie, it wasn't your fault and it wasn't Joe's fault so try not to dwell on it. And I don't think we need to tell that to Clay just now, it will only make it worse." Katie nodded.

The family waited together, taking turns going for coffee and/or snacks. Katie excused herself at one point and went to call Joe.

"Joe," she started calmly. "Do me a favor and call your friend Brad to see if he made it home okay. Will you do that for me please?"

"Yeah, sure. Okay, but why? Why would you care if he made it home, Kate? You can't stand the guy."

"My sister was hit by a drunk driver on Walnut Street, Joe. It could have been Brad. The driver that hit her is dead, Joe. So find out if your drunken ass friend is alive or dead. If he is alive, he's damn lucky." Kate hung up and went back to the waiting room with the rest of the family.

The surgeon who operated on Jessica came into the waiting room to address the family. He informed them that Jess had slipped into a coma. They all gasped. He went on to say that she had a fifty fifty shot of pulling through but the next twenty four hours should tell a better story. She could have some brain damage. Clay broke down and wept.

"Why don't you people go home and get some rest. This could take a long time, days or maybe weeks before we know the final outcome." The doctor offered his condolences and left.

Chapter 40

Since Jillian was small she had to stay in the hospital and be monitored until she reached five pounds. The first few days she lost a few ounces but Clay knew this was normal. She seemed to be doing well, all things considered.

Dr. Drake had his practice to tend to but he was only seeing patients who were sick and needed immediate attention. Two other pediatricians in town stepped in to help him with his patient load so he could spend time at the hospital with his wife and daughter. Days went by without any change in Jess' condition. Prognosis was not good.

The family all met over at Katie's house without Clay to discuss their options and to discuss what they could do to help Clay when baby Jilli was released from the hospital. After their meeting Emma and Bill went to see Clay at the hospital.

As they looked in through the window they could see Dr. Clay sitting in a chair beside Jessie's bed. He was holding her hand in both of his hands, kissing it, crying softly begging her to wake up. It brought Emma to tears and she had to go walk it off before entering the room. Bill let her go, giving her space. Her daughter may never wake up.

Clay saw Bill from the corner of his eye. He grabbed a tissue and left his wife's room.

The men greeted each other with a hug and a pat on the back. Emma came around the corner, wiping the tears away.

"Clay, we need to talk. Let's go down the hall and sit down," Bill suggested.

There was no one in the family waiting room so they went in and each took a seat so they could speak easily. Emma spoke first.

"We had a family meeting this morning. We know you can't take care of Jillian right now with your practice and Jessie like this, so we are here to help. We are family and we'll get through this, Clay." She paused to wipe a tear off her cheek.

She went on to tell him that Katie would take the baby and that she, Emma, would spend time at Katie's to help out. Donnie and Olivia also offered to take the baby but they felt that if Katie took her,

Clay could stop by any time to visit with his daughter.

Tears flooded Clay's eyes. He looked straight at Emma.

"I really appreciate that Emma but I just don't feel right entrusting our baby to Kate as long as Joe lives in that house. He's a drunk and his friend almost killed my family. I just don't trust him, Emma. I'll have to do something else, I'm sorry."

Clay put his head into his hands and cried.

Bill patted Clay on the shoulder. "Joe is out of the house Clay. He checked himself into rehab. He feels terrible about this. He will be away for six weeks and by then," his words drifted off as some new people entered the waiting room.

Emma saw the tension relax a little bit in her son –in law's face. She smiled. They walked to the nursery to see little Jillian. A nurse had just fed her and was about to put her back into the bassinette when she saw daddy and the grandparents at the window. She came out into the hall so daddy could hold his baby for a few minutes. She was absolutely the most precious thing Emma had ever seen. So tiny and yet, so perfect.

Clay had to leave to go do his office hours, he told them that he'd be back after his last patient. That gave Emma some time to be with her daughter. Bill went to the cafeteria after he walked Emma to Jessie's room. They needed time alone.

Emma got a face cloth and wet it and was washing her daughter's face while she talked to her as if she was wide awake.

"We just came from seeing Jillian, Jessie. She is the most adorable little thing you ever saw. Wait until you see her, Jess. I can just picture you now, dressing her up in tiny little foo foo dresses." Emma continued talking, not paying much attention, just washing her daughter to make her feel better, pushing her hair back from her forehead, washing each arm.

When she got to Jessie's hand, she stopped. She froze and stopped talking. Jess' fingers moved..Emma looked at Jessie's face and saw a smile begin to form on her daughter's lips, then her eyelids began to flutter open.

"Jessie!" Emma called to her. "Jessica baby. It's Momma, can you hear me Jessie?"

Emma rang the button for a nurse.

"I love you Mom," Jess whispered ever so softly. "Thank you for washing my face."

Emma burst into tears and bent over to kiss her little girl. A nurse came into the room and started to check the vital signs. She told Emma that she was going to call Jessica's doctor.

Bill came walking into the room, saw Jess' eyes open and almost dropped the two cups of coffee he was carrying.

"Oh well look who decided to wake up." He said with a big grin. "How do you feel, Jess?" He put down the coffee and hugged his wife.

"I feel a big groggy, like I've been asleep for weeks. Where's Clay?" Her voice was faint and hard to hear but Emma was surprised her daughter hadn't asked about her baby yet.

"He was here earlier but he needed to go check on some patients. I'll call him to come back." Emma reached for her cell phone.

Jess put her hand on her stomach and cried out loud. "My baby, Mom what happened? Where is my baby?" She was in a panic.

Jess remembered being in an accident but nothing else. She thought she was still pregnant. Then feared that she had lost the baby. She was freaking out when a nurse came into the room carrying Jillian.

"She's tiny, Jess, but she is fine honey," Emma took the baby from the nurse and pulled back the blanket to show Jillian to her Mother.

"Jilli," Jess said smiling, touching the tiny little face of her daughter. As much as she wanted to hold her baby, Jess didn't trust herself. She was still very weak and in pain.

Jess's doctor hurried into the room asking everyone to leave so he could examine his now wide awake patient. The nurse retuned Jilli to the nursery.

As they were about to go to the family waiting room to call Kate and Donnie, Clay rounded the corner, breathless. "Is it true? Is she awake and talking?" Emma cradled him in her arms.

"It's true, Clay. The doctor is with her now; give him a minute to check her over."

Kate was thrilled about Jess but she knew that she'd still need to help until Jessie got strong and back on her feet. She had a cracked rib and a fierce headache from the concussion. Emma tried Donnie's cell three times without a call back so she called Olivia's cell. It too went right to voice mail.

"You look worried, Emma. What's wrong?" Bill asked his wife on the way home.

"I can't get a hold of Donnie or Liv. Neither one is answering his phone. I didn't think Donnie looked good this morning at Katie's. He was coughing too much."

Bill agreed. He too noticed Donnie being out of sorts.

"He went outside twice that I saw," Bill explained. "He was choking, he was coughing so hard. I haven't seen him like that since he got his new lungs."

Emma nodded in agreement.

As Emma was clearing the table after dinner, her phone rang. "Olivia." She whispered to Bill as she answered.

"Hi Liv. I've been trying to call you and Donnie all day. Is everything okay?"

Bill watched the color drain from his wife's face as she listened to what her daughter in law was telling her.

"Oh God, Livvie. It's always something. What can we do to help?"

When Emma hung up she told Bill that on the way back from Katie's, Donnie had to pull over when he started to cough up blood. "Liv drove him to the closest ER and they sent him by ambulance up to Boston. She picked the kids up from school and dropped them off with a sitter and went in to see him. Her phone was off when I was calling."

She was going to text me a message but she knew we were in the hospital with Jessie. She just didn't want to add another burden on our shoulders.

"I told her we will always be there for her no matter what else is going on. Then I told her the good news about Jessie and she just burst into tears. She was so happy that Jess woke up and seemed to be doing okay. We were all very worried. I told Olivia that we'll be up there tomorrow, if you don't mind, Bill. I'd like to go with her into the hospital to visit Donnie and see what's going on with him. Perhaps you can stay with the kids if you would?" Emma knew he'd agree to anything she asked at this point. The stress factor was very high and she needed all support he could possibly give her.

The next day, having no knowledge that Donnie was back in the hospital, Clay called to say the doctor said Jessie is a miracle on wheels. "They got her up and she was weak but she walked a few steps, had a soft meal for dinner.

"The doctor feels that by the time Jilli is ready to be released, Jessie just might be strong enough to go home too." Clay was flying high. He was so grateful that both his wife and his new baby girl were going to be okay.

Emma told him then about Donnie being back in the hospital and that they were going to do a bronc on him. Either he had a bad virus or some rejection had invaded his body. Emma was going to go with Olivia to see him while Bill stayed at Donnie's with the kids. They had no school today. Clay wished them well. He said he'd tell Jessie when she was feeling a bit stronger and asked Emma to keep him posted on Donnie's progress.

When Emma and Olivia walked into his hospital room, they saw Donnie's doctor leave. He had just given Donnie the preliminary results of the tests they had done.

"My breathing level has dropped ten points and I have some rejection. They are going to treat it with some strong IV drugs and hopefully get me out of the woods. I'll be here for a few weeks." Emma heard the disappointment in his voice. He was pale and a little withdrawn. Even after six months, rejection can come at any time. He needed to be prepared for this. But he had been doing so well. It was discouraging.

Olivia just couldn't deal with it. She thought this was all behind them. She bent over him to hug him and began to cry.

"Liv, baby, please don't cry. We've talked about this. It happens, its normal," he patted her head. "I have new lungs but I still have Cystic Fibrosis. I'll bounce back; maybe I was pushing too hard? God isn't done with me just yet, but Olivia, don't ever forget, it's *INCURABLE!*

Rita Doyle Walsh grew up in the suburbs of Boston Massachusetts and now resides in Naples Florida with her husband and two small dogs.

Rita has published two other books also available on Amazon.com and at Barnes and Noble:

"SPLASH" and

"SPOILED LOVE"

Made in the USA
Charleston, SC
05 November 2015